Stolen Recipes
and
Saucy Stories

Best Girlfriends' Cookbook

Stolen Recipes
and
Saucy Stories

Best Girlfriends' Cookbook

Kay Morse

 **BookPartners**
Wilsonville, Oregon

BookPartners, Inc.
P.O. Box 922
Wilsonville, Oregon 97070

To all my girlfriends.

Acknowledgments

When deciding to write this cookbook I found myself so fortunate to have such good friends, girlfriends, who came to my rescue without a moments hesitation. Without their contributions, *Stolen Recipes and Saucy Stories* would have turned out to be a slim volume. I thank them all.

A hearty thank-you to Alan Churchill, Diane Bliquez, Linda Engebretsen and Ann Donley for their computer mastery.

My thanks to BookPartners for their guidance and support throughout the process — without their expertise, this work would have remained a spiral notebook sitting on my night stand.

I want to thank my two favorite men, my husband, Jim, and our two-year old Mitchell. Thank you both for your unending support.

Kay Morse

Foreword

"Food and friendship are twins; one without the other is a lonely thing."

Kay Morse

Perhaps more poems have been written about friends and more stories have documented the deep, magical bonds of friendship than any other subject — even love. It's the kind of magic that starts at kindergarten and goes to high school, to college, to weddings, and lasts beyond time. It has been said that all of life's achievements pale in the light of having gained a true friend, and that a queen's ransom cannot buy friendship. Just look at Shirley and Laverne, Thelma and Louise, Wilma and Betty, Lucy and Ethel and Charlie's Angels.

Some of the good times I've enjoyed with my best friends have taken place in the kitchen. Somehow, women end up gathering around the kitchen counter while the men head for the den or the patio. No matter how spacious the rest of the house, how lovely the hand-sponged walls of the living room, the life of the party begins and ends in the kitchen. I've been elbow-deep in mashed potatoes, buzzed around my kitchen in high gear, only to bump repeatedly into one of my chatty helpers. I love it; I wouldn't have it any other way.

We've all shared secrets while tossing a salad, pouring coffee or scrubbing pots. Bonds of friendship have deepened over a trip between the stove and the disposal. We've swapped stories, saucy and otherwise, toasted our friendship and created delicious meals. Friendship, along with food, adds up to the best of life's experiences.

From the time girls trade dolls, grow up to exchange lipsticks, clothes and secrets, share their hopes and dreams, bonds are forged that outlive time itself. But do these good friends share their favorite recipes? Well, some do, some don't. This book offers recipes that have been kept hidden by more than one generation, girlfriends' favorites, and several all-new and successful culinary creations. Some best girlfriends have been tricked, cajoled and threatened with a future of lumpy gravy into handing over their treasured secrets, while others had to be robbed of their recipes in the dark of night to bring the reader the best of all.

All in all, it has been great fun — stealing, borrowing and sharing my friends' tidbits and tales.

Kay Morse

Table of Contents

Alluring Appetizers

"A little of this and a dash of that create lasting friendship."

Kay Morse

A Worm-Eaten Cocktail Party

Reluctantly giving in to her husband's persistent badgering about having a cocktail party for thirty of his more or less business associates, and against her better judgement, Ann Howard set the date for the event with her husband Rick. Ann sent out clever little invitations, asking people to bring their spouses, and encouraging the singles to bring a date. When all the RSVPs were in, thirty people had accepted, dutifully informing their hosts they would bring a party buddy. Great! That added up to sixty people. Sixty! Wow! Ann made a stab at picturing that many guests in their home, which immediately reduced its spacious walls to doll-house dimensions.

Ann had never been fond of mass gatherings and agreed with the person who referred to these shindigs as "grazing on the hoof in overcrowded conditions." She also loved the words of the famous hostess Pearl Mesta, who fully believed that the same person who invented castor oil was responsible for creating the concept of the cocktail party.

Rick rolled his eyes back, and quickly nixed his wife's "great" idea of adding on to the house for the occasion. He was equally adamant about not engaging a caterer. He wanted just a simple, little get-together. Nothing fancy, you know!

Nevertheless, Ann purchased clever little napkins with clever little matching plates, and went about the business of planning what to serve, choosing what to drink, sorting through recipes for bits and treats, discarding this and adding that — and then did some more planning — all of which she found rather time-consuming.

A few hours before party-time, she arranged colorful tidbits on platters, assembled hors d'oeuvres, heaved dips and whips into serving bowls, added fruits and vegetables to cheese trays, made three large pitchers of martinis and stored it all in the refrigerator. Her daughter was around to give a hand here and there, while her ten-year-old son Ted was in the backyard digging for worms. He was going trout fishing with the Cub Scouts.

Showered, powdered and coiffed, Ann answered the doorbell which heralded the arrival of their first guests, and which continued to ding-dong until the house was stuffed to overflowing with people. Rick was circulating among his guests, filling wine glasses and pouring champagne. The dining room table with its candles and flowers was ready to be loaded down with food, and the hostess headed for the kitchen. She opened the refrigerator, and at the first glance decided to faint, but changed her mind and opted for death.

Strung across the fine rods of the metal shelves — row after row — were about three dozen fat worms with earth still clinging to their glistening forms. Another dozen or so had dropped off their perch and drowned in the martini pitchers. A few sturdy ones displaying signs of life were practicing swimming, but were most certainly too drunk to go fishing. The rest of her young son's worm collection wiggled enthusiastically over hors d'oeuvres, and a few sturdy ones were burrowing into one of the dips.

Ann closed her eyes, and she died — temporarily.

She doesn't remember what she did (or perhaps chooses not to). Ann just remembers her house was filled with people, and the walls reverberated with the sound of voices, chuckles, laughter and mindless chit-chat. There were compliments about the food — delicious, my dear, they said, and so appealingly presented. Oh, God, the food! And those people sipping martinis. Did she make a new batch? If she did, where did the gin come from? Ann thought she'd used it all up, or did she? Oh, dear — memory's gone; gone fishing.

All good things come to an end and so did the party. All that was left were wet stains on the formerly shiny surfaces of the antiques, spilled wine drying on white furniture, lumps of chips and dips ground into the now off-white carpet, Mindy in her mini sitting in the fireplace reading palms, Rick's best friend Fred curled up under the dining room table asleep with the family dog, and Ann's spirit dull and dented. Never, she swore to herself, under fire or threat of war, would she ever, ever, ever again....

And what about young Ted, you want to know? He's a good kid. He only followed his scout master's order to "store the worms in a cool and dark place."

Ingredients:

1/2	cup peperoncini peppers
1/2	cup cherry peppers
1/4	cup black olives, pitted
1/4	cup green olives, pitted
1/2	cup red peppers, roasted
1/2	cup artichoke hearts
5	tablespoons capers
1/4	cup olive oil
4	dashes Tabasco – or to taste

Crostini:

1	French baguette
1	stick butter, melted
1/2	teaspoon garlic powder

Stolen Muffalata Spread
On Crunchy Crostini

❋ Drain first 7 ingredients well; place in food processor, chop fine. Turn into bowl, add olive oil; correct seasoning with Tabasco. Place in serving container, offer with crostini.

❋ Crostini:

❋ Preheat oven to 350 degrees.

❋ Slice baguette 1/4 inch thick, place slices on cookie sheet. Combine melted butter with garlic powder; brush butter mixture on each slice. Bake at 350 degrees for 8 minutes, or until golden. Serve with muffalata or spread of your choice.

Taco Dip

Ingredients:

1   can (12-ounce) jalapeño refried beans

3   ripe avocados, cut into small cubes

Third layer:

1   cup mayonnaise

1   cup sour cream

1   package taco seasoning mix

2   cups cheddar cheese, grated

2   cups Monterey jack cheese, grated

7   green onions, chopped

1   large can (6 ounces net dry weight) olives, chopped

2   cans (4-ounce each) mild green chilies, chopped

2   cups lettuce, shredded

2   large tomatoes, chopped

❀ Each ingredient is its own layer, except for the third layer. The three ingredients for the third layer should be mixed together.

❀ Place each ingredient (in order, as listed) into a 9 x 13 inch glass dish.

❀ Chill for 2 hours and serve with tortilla chips.

Samos Island, Greece – July, 1988

Dear Diary:

Last night was not only wild but worthy of chalking up on my adventure score board. I shudder when I think how it could have turned out. Mary and I slept in the watchful company of a Greek army platoon on a sandy beach on Samos Island adjacent to the port.

It all started out with Mary and me arriving on schedule at the tiny port on quaint Samos Island, heading straight for the boat slips, certain that one of them would hold *Spontaneity,* our engineer-turned-adventurer uncle's sailing vessel. We looked and looked for the familiar lines of the boat whose bottom, top and sides we had sanded and painted as long as I can remember to earn our sailing time on her trim hull. We knew it wouldn't be any different on our trip to the Greek islands. Glamorous as it may sound to "sail the Greek islands," we would have to scrub and sand our way across the blue waters.

We waited the rest of the day, gazing out to sea, wishing and hoping to see the white sails of the *Spontaneity* approach the port and head for her slip. When it grew dark, Mary and I unstrapped our backpacks, ventured over to the café and ordered some feta, humus and pita bread along with the necessary glass of Ouzo. Finally, we went looking for a place to spend the night, only to discover that the one and only pensione in port was full. Back at the harbor, we turned a corner in the dark and found a soft, sandy beach.

We were both getting a bit more than apprehensive, and instinctively picked up a big rock each to fit our hands — a habit from childhood to ward off bad creatures, human or otherwise. We were about to jump out of our skin when a deep, male voice shouted something in Greek. We froze in our tracks as we saw a tall, dark shape approach our spot.

Mary shouted at the shadows that we were well-armed and not to come any closer.

In heavily accented English, a voice announced that the beach belonged to his "troops," and we were trespassing on army territory. The voice turned out to be a Greek soldier, with a flashlight and in the company of quite a few of his army buddies, who listened to our plight and invited us to spend the night on the beach with them. We had no place to go, and accepted their offer along with a pillow and a rough woolen army blanket. With our rocks clutched in one hand, and holding on to each other, we fell asleep a fair distance from our Samos Island Army Angels. (Mother would have fainted had she known of our circumstances —her precious twins, fresh out of college, on a dark night, in a foreign country, on a lonely beach full of handsome Greeks, etc., etc., etc.)

We slept uneasily off and on through the night, and were glad to see the sun rise. But, when it was all said and done, we were grateful for the Greek army's hospitality. Our angels took us to their barracks for a shower and strong coffee as well as a scenic tour of their station which sat high up on a cliff with a spectacular view of the west coast of Turkey. Two of our new-found buddies attached themselves to us and carried our packs on our hike back to the port in search of our elusive Uncle Doug.

What a welcome sight! There he was, arguing with the port authorities about the docking fee. With his business completed, introductions and hugs out of the way, true to form, Uncle Doug put us all to work sanding and scraping, including our army angels, rewarding us with generous amounts of sailor-made hummus and pita.

More tomorrow!

Easy Hummus with Warm Pita Bread

Ingredients:

1	can (14-ounce) garbanzo beans, drained
1/4	cup plus 2 tablespoons olive oil
1-1/2	teaspoons sesame oil
1/4	cup fresh lemon juice
2	cloves garlic, minced
3/4	teaspoon cumin
1/8	teaspoon salt
1/8	teaspoon pepper
2	tablespoons fresh parsley, finely chopped
1	package pita pockets

❀ Combine first 8 ingredients. Blend in food processor until creamy-smooth. Fold in parsley. Chill. Serve with toasted warm pita bread pieces. Makes about 1-1/4 cups hummus.

❀ To toast pita bread: brush pita pieces with a little olive oil and bake in 400 degree oven for 8 to 10 minutes. Cut into pie-shaped pieces.

Reuben Dip

Ingredients:

1	package (8-ounce) cream cheese, softened
1/2	cup sour cream
1	package (2-1/2-ounce) corned beef (thin-sliced lunch meat), cut into small pieces
1/2	cup sauerkraut
1	cup Swiss cheese, grated
1/4	teaspoon Worcestershire sauce
1/4	cup milk
2	large sourdough or rye cannonball rolls

❋ Preheat oven to 350 degrees.

❋ Combine first 7 ingredients. Hollow out one cannonball. Fill bread shell with mix, wrap tightly in foil and bake at 350 degrees for about 45 minutes or until hot and bubbly. Serve with bite-size pieces of bread made from inside of first cannonball loaf and second loaf.

Brie and Sundried Tomatoes

Ingredients:

2   medium-size wedges Brie
        cheese, top crust sliced off

Topping:
1-1/2	cups fresh parsley, chopped
1	jar (8-ounce) sundried tomatoes, drained, chopped
8	cloves garlic, chopped fine
2	tablespoons olive oil
1/2	teaspoon basil

❀ Mix topping ingredients together and microwave for 2 minutes on medium-high heat. Spread mixture over Brie; serve with crackers or thinly sliced, toasted French bread.

Powder Room Blues

Pam thoroughly enjoyed her so-called "clucking parties" when she lived in Virginia with her young family. Different faces at different times would appear on the Tacke household doorstep — all sweet women — all pretty, and all ready for some girl-to-girlfriend conversation. Husbands quickly retired to the television to watch that "important" ball game, discuss the latest whatever, while the women made their way to the kitchen where Pam had one of her delicious appetizers waiting. Pam has made her famous Blue Cheese Dip for years. Passed down from her mother Helen, it also doubles as dressing, to the delight of her guests. She arranges fresh vegetables in colorful clusters on a big platter around a bowl filled to the brim with her special dip, and the party is on.

One time there was a bit of a hitch during one of Pam's gatherings. Pam's children had recently acquired a new pet — a robin named Stanley, who had been tossed out of his nest during a thunderstorm into the thick ivy that climbed the side of the chimney. The young bird was flopping about on the patio, dazed and disoriented. Pam and the children took him in so he could recover from the ordeal, and named him Stanley. He soon had the run of the house. He wandered around, occasionally pecked on the refrigerator when he was hungry, and returned to his cage for a snooze quite content with his lot. He also liked to perch on curtain rods and light fixtures for a better look at his strange surroundings.

As the late afternoon wore on, one of Pam's guests ambled off in the direction of the powder room where, unbeknownst to her, Stanley was perched on the ceiling light fixture taking a nap. The poor lady quickly exited moments later, shrieking that some damn bird had dropped a sizable gift on her freshly coiffed hair. Poor Stanley! Frightened out of his wits with all the shrieking and ensuing commotion, he hurriedly winged his way back to his cage and stayed there for the rest of the evening, while mother tried to soothe her friend's ruffled feathers and rescue the hairdo at the same time. A glass or more of a fragrant Riesling, and frequent trips to the dip bowl, helped restore the all-around equanimity of body and soul.

Eventually, Stanley was released into the wilds of the family garden. In the beginning he returned occasionally to the window sill for some personal visiting, but soon forgot all about the Tacke family as he followed his bliss. Pam's powder room once again became a safe place to...powder one's nose, what else?

Ingredients:

1	quart top (Best Foods) mayonnaise
1	cup small curd cottage cheese
1	cup buttermilk
2	cloves garlic, finely chopped
8	ounces blue cheese crumbles

Blue Cheese Dip / Dressing

❋ Combine first 4 ingredients, beat smooth with a hand mixer. By hand, blend in blue cheese. Serve with your favorite chips and vegetables or use as dressing for mixed greens.

❋ Makes approximately 6 cups.

Grandma's Potato Chip Dip

Ingredients:

3	ounces cream cheese
1	pint small curd cottage cheese
1	dash Worcestershire sauce
2	cloves garlic, minced fine
1/4	cup milk
2	tablespoons fresh chives, finely chopped
	Salt and pepper to taste

❀ Mix all ingredients by hand. Refrigerate for 8 hours. Can be prepared a day ahead. Serve with your favorite potato chips.

❀ Makes about 3 cups.

Rosie's Roasted Pepper and Artichoke Tapenade

Ingredients:

1	jar (7-ounce) roasted bell peppers, drained, coarsely chopped
1	jar (6-ounce) marinated artichoke hearts, drained, coarsely chopped
1/2	cup fresh parsley, minced
1/2	cup Parmesan cheese, freshly grated
1/3	cup extra virgin olive oil
1/4	cup capers, drained
4	cloves garlic, chopped
1	tablespoon fresh lemon juice
1/8	teaspoon salt
1/4	teaspoon pepper

❀ Combine all ingredients in food processor. Blend until finely chopped. Transfer mixture to medium bowl. Cover and refrigerate. Serve with crostini (see Muffalata Spread recipe in index for Crostini recipe).

❀ Makes 1-3/4 cups. Can be prepared one day ahead.

A Hand Up – A Touchy Subject

There are situations in life where quick thinking and fast action override all codes of perfect behavior and propriety, even if this does turn Ms. Manners' hair gray. One such moment presented itself when we entertained some visitors from the east coast. Hollie and Greg were friends from college and our age, while the Hansons were in their late fifties, full of fun but quite dignified. A ride on our new boat was a perfect way to show off our city on a day when the sun turned everything golden, and the blue sky smiled down on our world.

We had recently completed a boat dock at our riverfront home, but had not yet begun work on the walkway that would eventually lead from the river bank up the steep rise to our house. Our river cruise having come to an end, we docked, secured the boat, and started the steep climb up the hill that ended in our backyard. Hollie and Greg headed up first, followed by Mr. Hanson, then Mrs. Hanson, my husband, and me as the caboose carrying our little boy.

Had anyone been around to take a picture of that mini assault on a mini mountain by six adults, lined up like a mountaineering group scaling Mount Everest *sans* ropes, the snapshot could have easily won first prize. Up the group scrambled, groping for holds on weeds and rocks in their struggle to reach the summit. Mrs. Hanson was having a hard time and had barely climbed ten feet when she began to slide back. She was about to collide — bumper to face — with my husband.

Instantly, I saw his hands fly upward and cup our distinguished guest's bottom, a hand on each cheek, as he pushed her uphill with all his might. I guess there is a literal meaning to to the words "bringing up the rear." Propelled by the hand-up, not looking back for a second, Mrs. Hanson climbed on, reached the top, straightened herself up, brushed off a few pieces of debris, and without a glance back at Jim asked in a slightly strained voice, "Young man, does your mother know what you're doing?"

Good-natured laughter broke out as we walked toward the deck where a chilled bottle of wine and some tempting appetizers were waiting. There's nothing like laughter along with some good food and drink to put things right.

Homemade Boursin

Ingredients:

8   ounces cream cheese, softened
4   ounces cottage cheese
2   large cloves garlic, pressed
1/4   cup fresh chives or green onion
       tops, finely minced
1/2   cup fresh parsley, finely minced
1/4   teaspoon freshly ground pepper
1/8   teaspoon salt

❀ Mix cheese in bowl with other ingredients. Blend well; refrigerate. Serve with your favorite brand of crackers. Recipe may be doubled. Low-fat cottage and cream cheese may be substituted.

A Dream Come True Down South

In the heart of the garden district of New Orleans sits the elegant Orleans Club. Behind its imposing doors, a grand staircase flows gracefully from the splendidly mirrored lobby to the upper floors. High ceilings lend a silent but haughty grandeur to the sparkling crystal chandeliers that shed their light on exquisite turn-of-the-century antiques adorning the venerable halls of this regal, old house. It is easy to picture lovely southern belles in silken hoop skirts on the arms of handsome young men waltzing in the glittering ballroom. This beautiful mansion was turned into a ladies club — a social place — and plays host to extravagant, magnolia-laden coming-out parties, important teas and sumptuous receptions.

Melissa had always been fascinated with the South — its history, its charm and the irresistible grace of its people. She envisioned herself a southern belle, strolling across the lawn of a plantation twirling her lace-trimmed parasol, playing croquet with good friends, and sipping iced lemonade in the cool shade of the deep porch, surrounded by a profusion of flowers and greenery. Her best friends all knew about her secret wishes, her dreams and her longings, and were delighted when she told them the good news.

Even though Melissa was more than a century removed from the Gone-with-the-Wind days, she did find her Rhett Butler. She married a proper southern gentleman in New Orleans, and her reception was held at The Orleans Club. For one night, she had her wish — she was a southern belle. There were dancing and music, laughter and happiness; the glitter of crystal and the rustle of full-skirted silk gowns. There were good wishes, rousing toasts, sparkling champagne and, of course, wonderful food served in handsome sterling silver chafing dishes, ornate trays and platters. For one night, the past had come to life and a young woman's dream had come true —Southern style.

Orleans Crab Dip

Ingredients:

1	package (8-ounce) cream cheese
1	stick butter
1	small bunch green onions, chopped
1	pound white crab meat, picked over
1 – 2	dashes Tabasco
1/4	teaspoon cayenne pepper

❀ In a medium-size skillet melt cream cheese and butter. Add chopped green onions, crab meat and seasoning. Sauté for 15 minutes. Serve in chafing dish to keep warm. Excellent with crostini or crackers.

Apple Caramel Dip

Ingredients:

1	jar (12-ounce) prepared caramel topping
16	ounces cream cheese, softened with 1 tablespoon milk
1/2	cup sugar
1	tablespoon dark molasses
1	teaspoon vanilla
5	Granny Smith apples, cored and sliced 1/2 inch thick
1	tablespoon lemon juice

❀ Melt cream cheese for 2 to 3 minutes in microwave on medium high in a glass dish. Mix sugar with molasses and add to cream cheese. Mix well. Add vanilla and stir well. Place in a bowl and drizzle caramel mixture over top.

❀ Cut and core apples and arrange on a platter. Drizzle lemon juice over apples to prevent from turning brown.

Cream Cheese–Gorgonzola–Walnut Spread

Ingredients:

8   ounces cream cheese, softened
6   ounces gorgonzola, softened
1/2   cup walnuts, coarsely chopped
2   cloves garlic, finely minced

❀ Combine cheeses, add walnuts and garlic, and stir by hand. Place on a platter or in a bowl and serve with an assortment of crackers.
❀ Makes about 2 cups.

Double Rejection

Catherine Gerlack is known for playing outrageous pranks on friends and family, and getting away with it. Somehow, she manages to draw her friends into her prankster schemes even though they swear that they will not again fall prey to her wacky games. She manages to remain one step ahead of her girlfriends, who with their eyes wide open, continue to be Catherine's innocent victims. I decided to turn the tables on her when Catherine submitted a recipe for her mother's Chinese noodles, expressing her hope that it would a be a good fit for publication in my *Stolen Recipes* cookbook. This was a golden opportunity for getting even; after all, as the saying goes, two can play the game.

In response to Catherine's submission, I played New York publisher and sent her a most professional-looking letter that went something like this:

Openhouse Publishing
333 Morgan Street
New York, N. Y. 10022

June 31, 1997

Dear Ms. Gerlack:

Thank you very much for favoring our publishing house with the submission of one of your recipes for our next cookbook, *Stolen Recipes and Saucy Stories.* Unfortunately, we deeply regret to have to decline your gracious contribution. As a matter of fact, we have included a second rejection slip just in case you ever get the urge to submit another one of your questionable Chinese concoctions, or any other kind to us again.

Sincerely, and with deep regret,

Megan Taylor, editor

encl.

This time the prankster was on the receiving end of the joke, and when all was told, she laughed good-naturedly, promised to reform, and handed over another recipe.

Won Ton Cups

Ingredients:

1	package won ton wrappers olive oil or canola mist (non-sticking spray)

Filling:

1	pound Monterey jack cheese, grated
1	cup sour cream
1/2	cup pitted black olives, chopped
1	can (7-ounce) mild green chilies, chopped
1	bunch green onions, trimmed, cleaned and minced
1	teaspoon ground cumin
1	teaspoon dried oregano
1	teaspoon curry powder

❀ Preheat oven to 350 degrees.

❀ Spray muffin tins with canola oil mist and place one wrapper in each cup. Mist each wrapper. Bake in oven until crisp, approximately 6 to 8 minutes. Remove cups from muffin tins, place on cookie sheet and fill.

❀ Combine all filling ingredients, and fill won ton cups with 2 tablespoons of mixture. Bake for about 6 to 8 minutes, until filling is hot and bubbly.

❀ Makes about 30 to 40 won tons.

Toasted Basil Baguettes

Ingredients:

1/3	cup low-fat mayonnaise
1/2	cup Parmesan cheese, freshly grated
2	cloves garlic, pressed
1/2	cup fresh basil, finely chopped
1	French baguette, sliced 1/4 to 1/2 inch thick (about 24 slices)

❋ Preheat oven to Broil.
❋ Mix first 4 ingredients. Spread a little on each bread slice. Broil until topping is bubbly. Serve warm.

Two-Timing Trouble

After graduating from the university Maria Ponzi went to Italy for six months to study wine-making as well as marketing. She would be working in her parents' vineyard, which produced some of the best wines in Oregon. Maria loved Italy, but wished secretly that she didn't have to leave her fiancé behind. Much in love, the young couple wrote to each other daily, and spoke on the phone frequently.

Meanwhile back home, Melissa, a young woman of Maria's age, met an attractive, pleasant man and fell head over heels in love with him. Joe Schamo quickly became the light of her life. A few weeks into the romance, Joe professed his love for Melissa over a dinner of cheese-stuffed ravioli accompanied by a ruby-red Merlot. He asked her to marry him. With the glow of the wine and Joe's proposal warming her body all over, she accepted, and went about planning her wedding, though no date had been set.

Maria returned to Oregon, fell happily into the arms of her fiancé, started her career in the family wine-making business, and went to work on her wedding plans. Her days were full, so were her fiance's, and the couple's social life took a backseat to their business activities. Getting a bit lonely for some fun, Maria accepted an invitation to a tailgate party from her alma mater, celebrating the first football game of the season. Her beloved informed her sadly that he had a previous commitment — a conflict of dates — and would be (sad, sad, sad) unable to escort Maria, who was looking forward to catching up with a lot of old friends at the event. Carrying a bowl of her favorite dip, she arrived at the scene.

Unescorted, Melissa also showed up at the party carrying her contribution to the event — a tray heaped high with spicy pickled shrimp. This she handed to the hostess at an old Ford station wagon, who was busily arranging food and drinks, and met Maria. The two young women took an instant liking to one another, chatted about this and that, and with plates in hand, helped themselves to some of the fabulous delicacies from the display on the station wagon's tailgate. Between bites, the conversation turned to Maria's wedding. The girls at the party, and especially Melissa, who was getting married herself, wanted to know every little detail of the wedding plans.

The two young women expressed regret at not having had an opportunity to meet each other before, and promptly set the date for the four of them to meet for dinner. In the meantime, they both spoke lovingly about their husbands-to-be. The more they chatted, the more striking the similarity of the men in their lives. It was uncanny!

Both were named Joe. Both were of medium height, had deep blue eyes and light-brown hair. They had graduated from the same school, had the same amount of siblings and, lo and behold, both worked as account executives for the same publicity firm. Wow! Life was certainly full of coincidences. Those boys even drove the very same car, loved big dogs and wore contact lenses.

When Melissa asked Maria if she would be changing her maiden name to that of her husband, Maria replied that she would keep her own, especially since her fiance's last name was Schamo.

"Schamo?" exclaimed Melissa — that was her fiance's name. The girls had more in common than a love for pickled shrimp; they had both fallen for the same man.

Needless to say, life giveth and life taketh. One day a man is loved by two women, the next day he has the love of neither.

Spicy Pickled Shrimp

Ingredients:

5	pounds large shrimp, cooked, deveined, shells removed
1	fresh lemon, thinly sliced
1	red onion, thinly sliced
1	cup black olives, pitted
2	tablespoons pimento, chopped
1	cup fresh lemon juice
1/2	cup oil
2	tablespoons red wine vinegar
2	cloves garlic, minced
1	bay leaf
2	tablespoons dry mustard
1/2	teaspoon cayenne pepper
2	teaspoons salt
2	teaspoons pepper

❀ Place shrimp, lemon, red onion, olives and pimento in a large bowl. In another bowl blend remaining ingredients well, pour over shrimp and toss. Transfer shrimp with liquid to large Ziploc bags and refrigerate overnight. Before serving, place in a decorative bowl or container.

❀ Use toothpicks to serve.

❀ Serves 20 to 30.

Brazen Beverages

"A woman is like a tea bag — you can't tell how strong she is until you put her in hot water."

Nancy Reagan

Mañana Margaritas

The day Irene introduced Nina to the art of building and sipping sinful margaritas, she also told her friend about her first Mexican holiday. Settling back against the soft curve of her comfortable lounge chair, with an icy, lime-green Margarita in hand and a dreamy look on her face, she recalled the Mexican incident.

"I love just about everything that has anything to do with Mexico. I love the food, I love the drinks, I love the crafts, I am wild about chili feeds, margarita parties and mariachi bands and those little children with the big brown eyes. I love the people, the music, the sunny beaches, the flawless blue skies, and the mellow, laid-back, lack-of-rush approach to life.

"I'll never forget my first visit to Puerto Vallarta on our quest to escape the blustery February rains of our Northwest homeland. We had booked a room at an older oceanfront hotel and, immediately upon arrival, hurriedly changed our clothes and rushed to the uncrowded, sunlit beach where gentle breakers rolled in and retreated with soft rushing sounds. We settled in with our beach gear near a group of three deeply-tanned men and two women, who were stretched out in the sun in what seemed a comfortable silence.

"Without opening his eyes, one of the men yawned, took a deep gulp of ocean air and said to the world in general, 'That was a good bullfight yesterday [Wednesday].'

"Silence. Quite a few minutes passed in silence, then one of the women said lazily, 'The bullfight wasn't yesterday, it was three days ago.' (She meant Monday.)

"A voice slower than honey flowing off a spoon replied with a touch of exasperation, 'You're both wrong, the bullfight was one week ago today.' (She meant Thursday.)

"Slowly, the second man opened his eyes, raised himself on his elbows and with conviction announced, 'Wrong, wrong! The bullfight will be tomorrow, which means the last one was six days ago.' With that he turned his face back to the sun. He thought it was Saturday.

"My orderly mind couldn't stand it any longer. I turned my head and addressed the group in an almost scholarly fashion. 'I hate to tell you this, ladies and gentlemen, but today is Thursday, and that means the bullfight was four days ago, and the next one will be in three days.'

"Five heads slowly raised themselves from the backrests of their beach chairs and turned in our direction. Sunglasses were removed with an unhurried ease, and five pair of eyes checked out our winter-white limbs, scrutinized us thoroughly. Satisfied with what they perceived us to be — newcomer gringos — one of the darkly-tanned men raised his eyebrows, stifled a yawn, and in a voice laced with disgust bellowed accusingly, 'I...bet you know what year this is!'

"Saved by the appearance of the hotel waiter with a tray full of cool margaritas, we immediately deployed them as a sort of peace offering to the group. We had a good laugh, started to chat with them, were turned on to the local customs, made a date for the next bull fight (Sunday!), and for the remainder of our first Mexican holiday spent most every day in their delightful company. The day we left our carefree beach, I had forgotten my maiden name and couldn't recall my birth date. I did fit right in. No wonder I love Mexico—you just don't get any older. Nobody knows what time it is!"

Mañana Margarita Mix

Ingredients:

6	ounces good tequila
4	ounces triple sec
1/3	cup frozen limeade concentrate (approximately half a small can)
2	cups ice
1	egg white

❀ Combine all ingredients in blender, blend until frothy.
❀ Serves 6.

Bermuda Rum Swizzlers

Amy and Brian spent their honeymoon in Bermuda. During their stay, the honeymooners wanted to snorkle around a beautiful and well-known reef. They joined another couple on a fast, sleek speedboat that would take them to their destination, a good distance away from the golden beaches of Bermuda.

The first mate on the boat, a salty but quite distinguished older Englishman, produced pitcher after pitcher of rum swizzlers with irresistible regularity. The fresh fruit juices and crushed ice somewhat dulled the presence of rum, which made the contents of the tall, frosted glasses a welcome thirst-quencher. What with the warm sun and the sea breezes, the demand for drinks never ceased, and soon it became evident that snorkeling was out of the question and would have to wait for another day. Instead, everyone opted for an extended boat ride on the calm tropical waters.

The two young couples thought they had gotten quite a bargain considering the generous rum swizzlers the English gentlemen dispensed, until their benefactor finally introduced himself. He turned out to be the CEO of one of the largest distilleries on Bermuda. He was the king of rum, he exclaimed, as he rolled back the sleeve of his designer shirt to expose the label of his famous brand of rum tattooed on his upper arm. So much for the reserved, tradition-bound English gentry.

Bermuda Rum Swizzlers

Ingredients:

4	ounces dark rum
4	ounces light rum
	juice of 2 limes
5	ounces pineapple juice
5	ounces orange juice
2	ounces grenadine
6	dashes bitters
4	cups crushed ice

❀ Place crushed ice in pitcher; add all ingredients. Stir or shake vigorously until a frothy head appears. Strain into glasses. May be served without being strained.

❀ Serves 6.

Hot Buttered Bum

He turned out to be a bum, but Melinda's heartstrings still pulled whenever Phil Liesaton's name passed her lips, long after he was found out. Phil was quite the boyfriend — he lived in a large, very old, white house in Pennsylvania that had a beautifully remodeled oval kitchen. Because he was a professional chef, his office was this kitchen, stocked with the latest gadgets and appliances, with impressive copper pots and pans dangling from a huge wrought-iron rack above his red, monster-size commercial range. Phil had one saving grace: he loved to cook, and was good at it. The good-for-nothing was actually good for *something*.

He experimented frequently with new recipes but rarely wrote them down. Whenever he did commit himself to paper, it was only temporarily, and after being dictated into his recorder, the pages were promptly placed in the paper shredder in his pantry. Some of his culinary secrets stayed in his devious little mind, but most of the recipes were recorded on tiny cassettes he kept in a lock-box tucked out of sight above the red range. Perhaps he just loved to hear the sound of his own voice.

The trouble started when Phil invited Melinda, along with a few friends, to spend a weekend at his beautiful country home. Several young women piled into Melinda's sedan, left Manhattan and drove to Pennsylvania one Friday afternoon in early October. They arrived just in time for a late dinner Phil had prepared. The meal was everything they had expected, and was topped by a wonderful, to-die-for dessert which their host served with great flair, along with steaming hot buttered rum in big mugs. The hot drink was so soothing and delicious that they had a second helping before retiring. That man could cook!

The next morning, everyone except Phil got up early, took a long walk through the countryside and luxuriated in all kinds of girl talk. The group returned to the house to explore the beautiful grounds with their manicured lawns and bursts of brilliant fall foliage.

They had just passed through the west lawn's garden gate, and turned into a grove of trees to witness a strange scene. They came upon Phil and his gardener Daisy Boobinski *in flagrante delicto*. Devastated that she had been betrayed, Melinda gave her fury free rein by flinging clumps of dirt at the offending lover, accompanied by a choice selection of curses and insults. Stopping short of spraying him with a nearby can of weed killer, she ended the two-year relationship between a bed of purple asters and a cluster of white chrysanthemums while Phil and Daisy, clumsily and red-facedly, disentangled themselves from their bed of petunias.

With Melinda in her friends' protective circle, the young women marched up to the house, dashed up the imposing staircase to the bedrooms, and packed their things. Melinda had disappeared for a short while, and met her friends at the car. Making the best of something gone bad, the little group of friends spent the entire drive home plotting the demise of Phil Liesaton, in ways which would have found favor in the eyes of a Spanish inquisitor.

When they finally turned silent, they noticed Melinda clutching something in her hand. When her friends asked if it was a piece of jewelry from Phil, or maybe the key to his house, her answer was No. But, with a vengeful grin of pure delight, Melinda opened her hand and revealed four small cassettes from Phil's well-guarded recipe collection. She had broken into his lock-box with a crowbar, and with all the strength of a woman scorned, stolen the cassettes and escaped out the front door undetected.

Back in Melinda's house, they popped the first cassette in the tape recorder, and heard Phil's pompous voice revealing recipe after recipe including his to-die-for "Mousse Mirabella" and the "Apres-Ski Hot Buttered Rum" that had captured their palates the night before.

Even though Phil turned out to be a lying, cheating Lothario, having absconded with a few of his recipes felt as good as having gained an important point in a debate, or having won a small war.

Hot Buttered Rum

Ingredients:

1-1/4	cups brown sugar
3	cups powdered sugar
2	sticks butter, softened
1	pint vanilla ice cream, softened
1/2	teaspoon all spice
1/2	teaspoon vanilla

Per serving:

2	tablespoons light rum
8	ounces hot water (to fill mug)
1	pinch nutmeg
2	tablespoons "buttered rum mixture"

❀ Combine first six ingredients with hand mixer.
❀ Can be stored in large container in freezer.
❀ To serve, place two tablespoons ice cream mixture in bottom of mug, add rum, hot water and nutmeg.
❀ Serves 25 to 30.

Ramos Fizz

There are drinks for all seasons and all tastes. Some drinks lose their popularity and fade away along with the days that created them, while others hang around for a good long time. To me, the Ramos Fizz represents an era that belongs to bouffant hair, beaded sweaters, and tropical attire from Abercrombie and Fitch. But to this day, bartenders still know how to fix that lighthearted, frothy drink.

Whenever I have a Ramos Fizz, I think back to the stories my parents told laughingly about their holidays in "old" Palm Springs, and their favorite spot, an exclusive enclave, the Smoke Tree Ranch. Mother wistfully recalls the many sun-drenched desert Sundays spent with friends in the shade of a smoke tree, sipping Ramos Fizzes — those deceptive milkshake-like drinks with a good kick. Getting fizzled on fizzes belongs to long-ago days, when life was more private, less frantic and a lot more gentle. I think I'll fix myself a Ramos Fizz.

Ramos Fizz

✻ Mix all in a blender. Serve in chilled glasses.

Ingredients:

Per person:

	juice of 1/2 lemon
1	egg white
1	scoop vanilla ice cream
2	ounces gin
1/4	cup crushed ice

Fireside Coffee

Ingredients:

2   cups instant hot chocolate
2   cups non-dairy creamer
2   cups instant coffee
1-1/2   cups sugar
1   teaspoon cinnamon
1/2   teaspoon nutmeg

❋ In a large bowl, combine all ingredients together with a fork. Divide into small, decorative jars as gifts, and give away! To serve, mix 1 heaping tablespoon of mixture into mug of hot water.

❋ Serves 100 or more.

Breakfast Smoothies

Ingredients:

1/2	cup nonfat milk
1/2	cup orange juice
1	cup (8ounces) plain or vanilla yogurt
1	banana
2/3	cup strawberries, fresh or frozen
1	tablespoon honey
3/4	cup ice cubes

✽ Frost glasses in freezer before serving.

✽ Place all ingredients in blender, mix until smooth.

✽ Makes 2 smoothies.

Bedside Breakfast Surprises

"Friends put the entire world to right over a cup of tea and a bun."

Charlotte Gray

The German Waffle Incident

Whenever Helen runs out of dinner ideas, she prepares a breakfast-for-dinner item, which is actually a favorite of hers, and carries with it a pleasant childhood memory. It reminds her of the evenings her mother picked up the gang after swim team practice, all tired and starving. Whenever she announced there was pot roast or stew for dinner, the kids would moan and groan, wishing they had snacked on a candy bar at least. But when their mother told them she had prepared breakfast-for-dinner, they couldn't wait to get home to those fragrant, crisp waffles or thick slices of French toast, and all the wonderful berries or jams, syrups and whipped butter they'd slather over their favorite food.

Now that she was married with one child, waffles for dinner though high on her personal list of favorites, lost ground to her husband's yearning for great French toast. And Helen's waffle iron died under strange circumstances.

The waffle iron in Helen and Jack's house was just about as old as their marriage and, just like their marriage, it worked fine. That is, until Gretel, their young helper fresh from her parent's small farm in Germany, was carried away by an all-consuming desire to have fat waves in her long, Teutonic-blond hair, which was as straight and as thick as the bristles on a broom. Another passion of hers — only matched by her undaunted curiosity — was her employer's gadget-filled kitchen, and her never-ending search for "what else this-thing-or-that might be useful for?"

Left to herself one afternoon, she had a brilliant idea — or so she thought. She divided her her two-foot-long tresses into several strands, wrapped each one in yards of clear plastic (using up a whole carton of that stuff), turned the waffle iron on high, placed a wrapped strand of hair in the waffle iron, closed the lid and "waffled" her hair. The act had nothing to do with German ingenuity or the advanced tech mind of youth. *Au contraire!* This kind of act goes back to the days of milking cows by hand.

Helen returned home and walked into the kitchen just as the waffle iron emitted hissing and spewing sounds. Clouds of evil-smelling steam rose from between the cracks where lid met bottom. Gretel let out a Valkyrie-like yodel, at the same time trying to extricate her waffling hair from the hot, sticky grip of the overheated appliance. Needless to say, the plastic wrap had melted, bonded to Gretel's fried hair and in the process, killed the appliance. What a mess!

Helen grabbed a pair of scissors, and disregarding the young girl's mournful howls and screechy protests, chopped off her hair at odd angles. By the time she finished, Gretel looked a lot more like Hansel. What happened to the waffle iron, you ask? Well, you already know — the family has been eating a lot of French toast lately.

Ingredients:

1	loaf day-old French bread, cut into 1-inch slices
5	eggs, beaten by hand
1-1/4	cups milk
1	teaspoon cinnamon
1	tablespoon orange peel, grated
3	tablespoons orange liqueur (or fresh-squeezed orange or tangerine juice)
1/2	teaspoon vanilla
2	tablespoons butter

Breakfast-for-Dinner French Toast

❀ In a medium-size bowl, beat eggs with milk; add remaining ingredients, except butter. One at a time, soak slices of bread in egg mixture.

❀ In a large skillet melt 2 tablespoons butter on medium heat. When butter is melted, add bread slices in batches. Fry on each side until golden brown. Serve hot. Add topping of choice.

❀ Serves 6 to 8.

❀ Topping suggestions: powdered sugar, berries, honey, maple syrup, fruit syrups, jams, whipped butter.

Orange-Sour Cream Coffee Cake Rolls

Ingredients:

Dough:

1	packet Fleischmann's active dry yeast
1/4	cup warm water
1/4	cup sugar
1	teaspoon salt
2	eggs, room temperature
1/2	cup dairy sour cream
6	tablespoons butter, melted
3	cups regular flour

Filling:

3/4	cup sugar
2	tablespoons orange rind, grated
2	tablespoons butter, melted

Glaze:

3/4	cup sugar
1/2	cup dairy sour cream
2	tablespoons orange juice
1/2	stick butter

⊛ Preheat oven to 350 degrees.

⊛ Dough:
⊛ In small bowl soften yeast in warm water. Stir in sugar, salt, eggs, sour cream and 6 tablespoons melted butter. Add half of flour, using electric mixer at medium speed. Gradually add remaining flour by hand. Cover, let rise in a warm place until light and doubled, about 2 hours.

⊛ Filling:
⊛ Combine 3/4 cup sugar and orange rind, and mix well. Set Aside. Knead dough on well-floured surface about 15 times. Roll out half dough to a 14-inch circle. Brush with 1 tablespoon melted butter and sprinkle with half of sugar and orange rind mixture. Cut into 12 wedges. Roll up, starting with wide end and rolling to a point — like a croissant. Repeat with remaining dough. Place rolls, point side down, in a well-greased 13 x 9 inch pan.
⊛ Cover with cotton tea cloth; let rise in warm place until light and doubled, about 1-1/2 to 2 hours. Bake at 350 degrees for 25 to 30 minutes, until golden brown. Leave in pan.

⊛ Glaze:
⊛ Boil ingredients for orange glaze for 3 minutes, stirring occasionally. Spoon orange glaze over hot coffee cake rolls. Best when served warm.
⊛ Makes 24 rolls.

Raw Apple Muffins

Ingredients:

4	cups Golden Delicious apples, peeled, diced
1	cup sugar
2	eggs, lightly beaten
1/2	cup corn oil
2	teaspoons vanilla
2	cups flour
2	teaspoons baking soda
2	teaspoons cinnamon
1	teaspoon salt
1	cup golden raisins
1	cup walnuts, chopped

❀ Mix sugar with apples and place in a medium sized bowl. Combine eggs with oil and vanilla and add to apple bowl. Combine all dry ingredients: flour, baking soda, cinnamon and salt, and add to mixture above. Stir well. Add raisins and walnuts and stir.

❀ Place in muffin tins that have been greased and floured or use paper cupcake cups in tins. Bake at 325 degrees for 25 to 35 minutes.

❀ Makes 16 regular-size muffins.

"Blue" Blueberry Muffins

Ingredients:

1	stick margarine, softened
1	cup sugar
2	eggs
2	cups flour
2	teaspoons baking powder
1/2	cup milk
1	teaspoon vanilla
1	cup whole blueberries, fresh or defrosted
1	cup whole blueberries, mashed

❀ Preheat oven to 375 degrees.

❀ Combine margarine with sugar and eggs, beat until smooth. Stir in flour and baking powder, add milk and vanilla. Fold in mashed berries and whole berries. Pour into greased muffin tins and bake for 30 minutes.

❀ Makes 24 regular-size muffins (about 12 jumbo muffins). Can double easily.

Memories

There are some places that leave a lasting impression on our minds. There are beaches one never forgets; a piazza in a certain light becomes imprinted somewhere behind one's eyes, and a sunset casts a lasting glow in one's heart. Friends meet and share memories of special places and treasured moments.

One of those places we discovered is a bed-and-breakfast inn, nestled on a green hillside with a wide river rolling by. Whenever some of us girls feel like running away from home — to get together, woman to woman, and catch up with each other, we head for the Swift Shore Chalet Bed and Breakfast in West Linn, Oregon.

The great view, the soothing sounds of the rushing river, the serene garden setting, and the attentive care of the innkeepers have kept a bunch of us girlfriends coming back again and again. We forget about the cares of the world for a while, swap tales and tidbits and leave renewed, refreshed and recharged with promises to meet again — same place, same time.

Swift Shore's Mandarin Orange Scones

Ingredients:

1-3/4	cups flour
2	tablespoons sugar
1-1/4	teaspoons baking powder
1/4	teaspoon baking soda
1/2	teaspoon salt
6	tablespoons butter (3/4 stick)
1/2	cup buttermilk
	zest of one orange (save 1 teaspoon for glaze)
1	can (11-ounce) Mandarin oranges, drained and chopped (save 8 mandarin slices for garnish)

Glaze:

1	cup powdered sugar
1	teaspoon reserved orange zest
	enough juice from orange to make glaze consistency (about half of orange)
3	drops orange flavoring

❀ Preheat oven to 425 degrees.
❀ By hand, mix dry ingredients, cut in butter until dough is pea size, add buttermilk, chopped mandarin orange pieces and orange zest. Dough will be sticky. Turn out onto well-floured board, add flour as needed to make manageable. Knead lightly a couple of times and form into 8-inch round. Place round on greased cookie sheet. With a spatula, score eight wedges on the round and bake for 12 to 16 minutes or until golden brown. Remove from oven and glaze.

❀ Glaze:
❀ Combine powdered sugar, zest, orange flavoring and enough freshly squeezed orange juice to make a runny glaze. Pour glaze over rounds; garnish each wedge with one mandarin slice.
❀ Makes 8 scones.

The Yogurt Parfait Affair

Suzanne was quite the hostess. She loved to give a party at the drop of hat, or any other reason for that matter. Shortly before her good friend Julie's baby was due, Suzanne arranged a baby shower in her home for the expectant mother and invited about twenty of their "best" girlfriends. No different from all the other events in her home, Suzanne's party started out to be a huge success, except for the fact of a peculiar happening.

Just as Suzanne's guests were about to attack the tall glasses filled to the brim with a delicious "Yogurt Parfait," and were getting ready to present Julie with her baby gifts, Tiffany's purse rang. She quickly grabbed her cell phone, and dashed off to the kitchen to answer her call in privacy. Moments later, she returned to the group, tearfully informing everyone that her mother-in-law had been stung by a bee while working in her garden. The poor woman had suffered a severe allergic reaction. Covered in potting soil and still wearing her gardening gloves, she was taken by ambulance to St. James Hospital. The distraught young woman gave quite a performance of distress and concern, and managed to make the rest of her friends fear for the life of the bee-stung victim.

Dabbing at her eyes, Tiffany stuffed the phone back into her big purse, said a hurried goodbye, and dashed out of the house, only to return seconds later asking the other guests to move their cars. Her sharp little sportscar had been the first to park on Suzanne's long, but narrow, packed-dirt driveway, and was hemmed in by a string of Suburbans, sedans and mini-vans. Suzanne knew her driveway could be quite a nuisance and somewhat of a harrowing experience when maneuvering a vehicle back onto the road in reverse. She rushed out of the house to direct traffic.

The guests rose to their feet, grabbed car keys and stood in line to move the ten automobiles that were impeding Tiffany's getaway. It took quite a while to jockey the vehicles onto the road and, after Tiffany's departure, drive them back into position on the driveway. Everyone was relieved to see the taillights of her car disappear as the distraught woman headed to the bedside of a critically-ill member of her family. The shower party returned to the house to finish their by then warm parfaits, and discuss poor Tiffany's mother-in-law.

Suzanne spoke to Julie the following day, inquiring if there had been any news about Tiffany's mother-in-law. Well, Julie took a deep breath and gave out the news.

The story about the mother-in-law, the bee sting, the garden gloves, the ambulance, etc., etc., etc. had been a huge lie. The call Tiffany *had* received had been from her married lover, asking her to make a beeline for a different kind of get-together than an all-girl shower, taking advantage of the fact that both their spouses were out of town.

The moral of the story: Beware of the sting of the bee, or better yet, the sting of the lie.

Yogurt Parfait

Ingredients:

1/2	cup low-fat granola, divided
1	cup vanilla yogurt, divided
1	teaspoon honey (to be drizzled over yogurt)
1/2	cup fresh strawberries, chopped, divided (peaches, apricots or dried fruit may be substituted)

❀ Using each ingredient as a layer, in a glass dish or large wine glass, divide ingredients and create two layers of each, ending with fresh fruit. Garnish with a sprig of fresh mint.

❀ Serves 1.

Vacation Egg Casserole

Ingredients:

3	cups frozen shredded hash brown potatoes, shredded or diced
1	cup Monterey jack cheese, shredded
3/4	cup fully cooked ham or Canadian bacon, diced
1/3	cup green onion, sliced
4	eggs, beaten
1	can (12-ounce) evaporated milk, regular or skim
1	can (4-ounce) mild green chilies
1/4	teaspoon pepper
1/8	teaspoon salt

❋ Preheat oven to 350 degrees.
❋ Grease a 2-quart baking dish; arrange potatoes evenly in bottom of dish. Sprinkle with cheese, ham and green onion. In a medium-size mixing bowl combine eggs, milk, chilies, pepper and salt. Pour mixture over last layer. May be covered at this point and refrigerated for several hours or overnight. Bring to room temperature; bake, uncovered, for 40 to 45 minutes, or until center appears set. Let stand for 5 minutes before serving.
❋ Serves 6 to 8.

Rites of Passage

Girlfriends not only find excuses to get together, but in doing so, assure the survival of a friendly social custom which offers unlimited opportunities for keeping in touch, celebrating each other, and furthering the ritual of creating delicious dishes.

These events include the hallowed traditions of baby showers, wedding showers, book club gatherings, neighborhood cleanup lunches, meetings, etc. Between conversations, girlfriends have a chance to sample the selection of foods prepared by the hostess. Whenever Meredith is in charge of a breakfast gathering, she sticks to her favorite menu: fruit salad with a berry yogurt, toasted bagels with various cream cheese spreads and her standby fail-safe frittata. Always a crowd pleaser, it is an egg casserole with a fancy nineties name. It is simple and delicious, and offers the hostess an opportunity to take part in the visiting, because the dish is prepared in advance — tossed in the oven for quite a while, and then served. Meredith doesn't have to spend her time in the kitchen while her guests are having fun.

Fail-Safe Frittata

Ingredients:

4	medium potatoes, peeled and sliced
1/4	cup olive oil
1-1/4	cups yellow onion, chopped
1/2	cup red pepper, chopped
4	cloves garlic, minced
2	cups broccoli, fresh or frozen, chopped
14	eggs
1	cup Parmesan cheese, grated
2/3	cup water
1	teaspoon dry basil
1/2	teaspoon salt
3/4	teaspoon pepper
1-3/4	cups Monterey jack cheese, shredded

❀ Preheat oven to 350 degrees.

❀ In a large skillet sauté potatoes in olive oil for 20 minutes on medium heat. Add onion, red pepper and garlic, cook until onion is tender, about 10 minutes. Add broccoli, cover and cook for 4 to 6 minutes. In a separate bowl, combine eggs with Parmesan cheese, water, basil, salt and pepper. Turn skillet contents into a 4-quart baking dish. Pour egg mixture over potato mixture. Top with shredded Monterey jack. Bake for 35 to 40 minutes.

❀ Can be prepared ahead, refrigerated and baked the next day.

❀ Serves 8 to 10.

Swiped Salads

It's certain that fine women eat a crazy salad with their meat.

William Butler Yeats

For Married Women Only

  Weekends at Hayden Lake, Idaho were times spent in heaven for ten sorority sisters. Lyn Peterson's parents were the perfect parents and hosts who gave the girls the run of their lakeshore place, guesthouse and all. Between taking turns at water skiing in the early morning hours, and getting dumped in the icy waters of the lake, the girls warmed up with cups of steaming hot coffee while wrapped in big, soft beach towels. Trying to sit at the water's edge as a bystander wasn't in the plan. Mr. Peterson insisted everyone have a turn, regardless of the hostile water temperature.

  The long weekends were real girl-to-girl events — borrowing each other's clothes, lipstick and bathing suits, going on boat rides, taking long walks and talking long into the night.

  Lyn's mother, Jackie, prepared delicious meals, including a very special salad. "Jackie's Salad" instantly became a favorite of the Pi Phi girlfriends, who asked their hostess for the recipe. However, no amount of pleading would budge Jackie into handing it over. Weekend after weekend, year after year, the answer to their requests remained a staunch "NO." However, Jackie promised to send the recipe to each one of the young women on her wedding day — and so she did. Along with her good wishes and a gift, she included a copy of her famous salad recipe. The girls all promised to keep the recipe secret; well, most of them.

Jackie's Spinach Salad

Ingredients:

1   bag (10-ounce) baby spinach (about 8 cups), cleaned
1   head butter lettuce, cleaned and torn into bite-size pieces
1   large or 2 small avocados, sliced
1   bunch green onions, chopped
2   bananas, cut into 1/2-inch slices
1   pint fresh strawberries, sliced

Dressing:
1/3   cup white wine vinegar
1   cup vegetable oil
3/4   cup sugar
1/2   small red onion
1   teaspoon dry mustard
1   teaspoon salt
2   tablespoons poppy seeds

❀ Blend all dressing ingredients but poppy seeds in food processor on medium speed until well mixed. Fold poppy seeds into dressing mixture by hand. Toss salad ingredients with dressing just before serving.
❀ Dressing can be prepared 2 days ahead.
❀ Use a variety of your favorite salad greens if you do not favor spinach. Add shrimp or chicken to make an entrée salad.
❀ Serves 8 to 10.

Ingredients:

8	cups mixed wild greens
1	Granny Smith apple, sliced thin
1/2	cup almonds, slivered and toasted
1	cup dried cranberries
1	yellow pepper, thinly sliced
1	orange pepper, thinly sliced
1	cup crumbled blue cheese

Dressing:

1/3	cup olive oil
1/3	cup balsamic vinegar
3	tablespoons orange juice
1/2	teaspoon sugar
1	teaspoon basil
1	teaspoon oregano
1	clove garlic, minced
1	tablespoon black pepper

Special Mixed Green Salad

❀ Buy 1 bottle Jaipur Dressing by Black Swan. If you can't locate this dressing, call Black Swan Inc. at 1-800-228-8954, or try gourmet grocery stores in the produce section (there are no preservatives in it). Following dressing serves as a good substitute.

❀ Combine all salad ingredients together in a large bowl. Mix all dressing ingredients; pour over greens. Toss.

❀ Serves 6.

Kitchen Sink Salad

Ingredients:

Base salad:

10	cups Continental Salad Blend in a bag, or other greens
1/2	red onion, sliced into bite-size pieces
1	can (12-ounce) mandarin oranges, drained
6	ounces feta, goat or bleu cheese, crumbled
3/4	cup walnuts or candied pecans
3/4	cup dried cranberries

Optional:

1	can black olives, pitted, whole
1	jar (6-1/2-ounce) marinated artichoke hearts, cut into bite-size pieces
1	small can baby corn, cut into bite-size pieces
1	cup mushrooms, thinly sliced
1	can (9-ounce) garbanzo or kidney beans
1	tablespoon fresh basil, chopped
1	tablespoon fresh oregano, chopped

Dressing (or use any vinaigrette):

1	cup olive oil
1/2	cup red wine vinegar
3	large cloves garlic, minced fresh ground pepper to taste

❋ Tear lettuce into bite-size pieces and place in a large salad bowl. Add all ingredients to bowl, dress and toss well.

❋ Feel free to add any of the optional items.

❋ Serves 8.

The Salad Whisperers

There is no doubt in my mind that all kinds of information come to us in all sorts of peculiar and, more often than not, strange ways. Some sources are forever kept secret, others are too embarrassing to remember, while still others beg to be shared with the world, for no better reason than to laugh about it. Such is the case with Liza's story about her favorite salad fixings.

Liza was toweling off from her shower at the uptown athletic club, when she noticed two stark-naked women huddled behind the last row of lockers, conversing in subdued voices with an air of top-secret-for-your-ears-only about them. Liza, never having abandoned her Eve-like Garden-of-Eden curiosity, dropped her towel thoughtlessly on the floor and, in her birthday suit, sidled up to position herself at a more advantageous listening post in order to overhear the hushed conversation. It had to be something good, she hoped — no doubt it was a bit of juicy gossip about a club member.

But all she heard was a reciting of ingredients for a salad. At first disappointed about not hearing something more exclusive or naughty, she then considered the fact that perhaps the recipe in question might be something out of this world, since the ingredients were conveyed to another person in such a clandestine manner.

Just then one of the women asked her compadre to repeat the ingredients, and Liza tiptoed back to her locker, grabbed a pen and scrap of paper from her purse, and rejoined the salad whisperers in time to take down the secret formula.

It was only afterwards, with the stolen recipe safely tucked away in her purse and a full set of clothes on her back, that Liza realized what an absolutely ridiculous picture the three naked women must have made had someone come upon the scene: two nudes huddled on the ladies' locker room floor whispering, and a third nude pressed flat against an open locker, hidden from view by a row of lockers, furiously taking notes.

This was a paparazzo's dream come true. What a grand exposé it could have been for the pages of the club's winged newsletter.

Whisper Salad

Ingredients:

1   tablespoon olive oil
1   clove garlic, finely minced
1   can (15-ounce) lima beans, drained
1   can (15-ounce) garbanzo beans, drained
1   can (15-ounce) sweet corn, drained
1   can (8-ounce) water chestnuts, whole
1/2   cup cilantro, finely chopped
3   Roma tomatoes, chopped
1/4   teaspoon salt
1/4   teaspoon pepper

❀ Over low heat, lightly sauté garlic in olive oil. When bubbly, add beans, corn, and water chestnuts; heat thoroughly until warm (about 5 minutes). Remove from heat. Add cilantro and tomatoes and toss. Sprinkle with salt and freshly ground pepper.

❀ Serves 4.

Chicken Salad and Twists

Ingredients:

8	ounces rotelle pasta
1/2	cup sesame seeds, toasted
1	cup vegetable oil
2/3	cup soy sauce
2/3	cup white wine vinegar
6	tablespoons sugar
1	teaspoon salt
1/2	teaspoon pepper
3	cups cold cooked chicken, shredded
1/2	cup parsley, chopped
1/2	cup green onions, sliced
8	cups spinach leaves

❀ Cook rotelle al dente and drain well. Let cool. Combine sesame seeds, oil, soy sauce, vinegar, sugar, salt, and pepper. Pour over cooled pasta. Add chicken and toss gently. Cover and chill until next day. To serve, add parsley, onions and spinach. Toss lightly.

❀ Serves 6 to 8.

Garbanzo Beans Gone Bad

Eating a vending-machine lunch at one's desk was considered "normal" in the fashion-buying office of a large department-store chain. *Chez Desk* was not Laila's favorite restaurant, so she gladly accepted an invitation to join several of her colleagues on a rare visit to a real restaurant to celebrate the boss's birthday.

She ordered the vegetarian house specialty, a tangy couscous-garbanzo bean salad, which she enjoyed to the last bite. Unbeknownst to her luncheon companions, Laila had been thinking of an excuse to leave work early that day to interview for a job with another company. Having used all of her time off for the year, she was left with only one solution, to feign illness. Suddenly, she came up with the perfect plan — blame her "illness" on the meal she had just devoured. Food poisoning was a believable way out.

Before the plates were cleared, Laila started to moan. With suffering written all over her face, she clutched her stomach and groaned repeatedly. She excused herself and ran off in the direction of the ladies' lounge, and, to the surprise and concern of the rest of the luncheon party, Elizabeth, a fashion coordinator, clutched her napkin to her mouth, made a strange gurgling sound, rose from her chair and followed Laila's footsteps.

It wasn't long before both women emerged from the powder room, announced to the luncheon party they were ill, and blamed their condition on the house special. The boss quickly excused the duo, and insisted that they go home at once. The restaurant manager, aware of the commotion, felt terrible that two customers had gotten sick and took care of the entire bill.

Once outside, Laila and Elizabeth hurried to the parking lot, climbed into their respective cars and drove off in different directions. Laila arrived at her destination in due time, checked in with the receptionist, took a seat and waited to meet with her interviewer. Just then the door to the outer office opened, and guess who walked in? There was Elizabeth, no longer clutching a napkin to her mouth, no longer grabbing at her middle, but looking hale and hearty, applying for the same job. The two friends looked at each other for a moment and broke out laughing — two souls and one mind.

Couscous and Garbanzo Bean Salad

Ingredients:

1-3/4	cups water
1/2	teaspoon salt
1	cup couscous
1	can (15-ounce) garbanzo beans, drained
2	small red bell peppers, diced
4	green onions, thinly sliced
1/2	cup Kalamata olives, diced
1/2	cup carrots, finely chopped

Mint Vinaigrette:

3/4	cup leafy fresh mint sprig tops, finely chopped
3	tablespoons white wine vinegar
1	clove garlic, minced
1	teaspoon Dijon mustard
1/4	teaspoon sugar
2/3	cup olive oil
6	ounces feta cheese, crumbled

❋ Bring water and salt to boil in medium saucepan; add couscous. Remove saucepan from heat; cover and let stand for 5 minutes. Transfer couscous to large bowl.

❋ Fluff with fork. Add garbanzo beans, red peppers, green onions, olives and carrots.

❋ Mint Vinaigrette:

❋ Blend mint with vinegar, garlic, mustard and sugar in food processor; add olive oil and blend well.

❋ Toss vinaigrette with couscous mixture. Add feta cheese and toss once again.

❋ Can be prepared 6 hours before serving and is still good the next day.

❋ Serves 4 to 6.

Blanche's Potato Salad

Ingredients:

10	baby red potatoes with peel left on
8	green onions, chopped
7	boiled eggs
6	tablespoons mayonnaise
	salt to taste

❀ Boil potatoes until fork-tender, approximately 20 minutes. Cool potatoes and cut into small chunks. Cool boiled eggs, peel and cut all but one egg into chunks. Mix potatoes, chopped onions and eggs. Fold in mayonnaise and add salt to taste. Transfer to serving bowl. Slice remaining egg and use as garnish.

❀ Serves 4.

Crunchy Cabbage Salad

Ingredients:

Salad:

1/2	head cabbage, finely chopped
2	teaspoons sesame seeds, toasted
1/2	cup sliced almonds, toasted
4	green onions, chopped
1	package Ramen noodles (chicken flavor - Maruchan recommended)

Dressing:

2	teaspoons sugar
1	tablespoon vinegar
1/2	cup vegetable oil
1/2	teaspoon pepper
1	package Ramen chicken seasoning

❁ Toss first four salad ingredients together. Combine dressing ingredients in separate bowl. Salad and dressing can be refrigerated at this point. Just before serving crunch dry Ramen noodles into small bits and add to cabbage mixture. Toss with dressing.

❁ Serves 4.

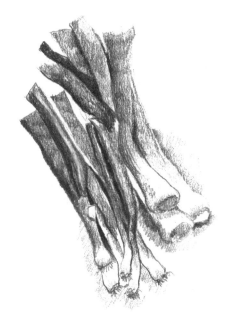

Blush My Soul

Cindy's girlfriends no longer ask for a glass of red wine when visiting their friend's home, unless she decides to have her house decorated in shades of burgundy. The danger of upsetting a tall-stemmed glass with a careless motion is always at hand.

During a party, some time ago, one of Cindy's friends knocked a glass of "deep red" off her coffee table. Its contents splashed a crimson path on the beautiful white silk curtains in the living room, and played red-hot havoc with a white silk-covered chair.

Cindy's husband instantly whisked away the chair and placed it in the shower for a hosing down. The curtains were quickly yanked off the rods, and left to soak in the guest bathtub. Where was Heloise when Cindy needed her? Well, there's a first time for everything. No one had the slightest idea of what to use for removing the terrible stains.

Lemon? Vinegar? Soapy suds? It was all guesswork. There wasn't much anyone could do, and Cindy didn't want to spoil the evening by moaning over spilled wine.

The group picked up the conversation and helped themselves to generous portions of a great salad, hoping that some magical cleaning service would have the answers to the dilemma, or dye the damaged goods a deep color, perhaps purple or red would be safe from her hand talking friend.

Imitation Lord Fletcher's Salad

Ingredients:

1	large head iceberg lettuce, torn into large bite-size pieces
1	cup soy bacon bits
1/4	large purple cabbage, cut into large bite-size pieces
1	cup Girard's Caesar salad dressing

❀ Combine all ingredients and toss together just before serving.
❀ Serves 4 – 6.

Chinese Broccoli Salad

Ingredients:

2	pounds broccoli florets, cut into 2-inch spears
1	red pepper, sliced into thin 2-inch strips
1-1/2	cup walnut halves

Dressing:

1	tablespoon garlic, crushed
1/3	cup safflower oil
1	tablespoon Chinese sesame oil
1	tablespoon soy sauce
1	teaspoon salt
2	tablespoons fresh lime juice
1-1/3	cups rice vinegar
1	tablespoon ginger root, freshly minced
1	cup fresh mushrooms, cleaned, stems removed

❈ Combine all dressing ingredients and chill. Steam broccoli approximately 15 minutes. Rinse with cool water and drain. To serve, place broccoli, red pepper and dressing in salad bowl and toss. Add walnuts.

❈ Serves 4 to 6.

Steamy Soups

"God gives us relatives; thank God we can choose our friends!"

Ethel Watts Mumford

Chicken Soup For the Tailbone

Lori was a guest at her friend's rambling old house, near a noisy highway and close to the medical school Dan and his roommates attended. She had been invited to the end-term party the young doctors-to-be had thrown the night before, helped clean up the remains of the festivities, and rather than driving across town, decided to spend the night in a spare room in the attic.

She woke up in the early morning hours looking for a bathroom. Not having a robe along, she wrapped herself in her blanket and tiptoed down the hall to the stairs that led to the lower floor and the only working facility. The hall was dark and cluttered with all kinds of stuff, attesting to the lack of housekeeping skills the occupants displayed.

Lori tripped, slipped at the top of the stairs, bounced down the unfriendly staircase, not missing even one of the fourteen steps, and landed in a pitiful heap at the bottom of the stairwell. She had lost her blanket at the top, and there she sprawled, unable to move, in her altogether in an all-male residence.

She heard several voices, as the young doctors responded to the thundering bumps her body had made as it connected with the sharp wooden edges of each and every stair. They might consider a burglar was at work and check it out! Terrified to be discovered in her awkward position, she shouted to be left alone, assuring everyone she was all right. It took a few moments for Lori to realize she was not all right, and would need medical attention. She finally called out for someone to bring her a robe and call 911.

An ambulance arrived, and she was whisked off to the university hospital wearing a borrowed robe and sporting a very sore bum. She was not able to move as she underwent long hours of unpleasant examinations and endless X-raying. She was finally told she had broken her tailbone. The damage was permanent and far-reaching. Sitting on a foam cushion for the rest of her life was not nearly as threatening or as serious as the fact that natural childbirth was out for her.

Instead of undergoing surgery to remove the broken bone, she opted for three weeks of bed rest to allow for the bruising to subside and the intense pain to end. Released to the loving care of her mother, Lori's bottom healed nicely — what with all that wonderful White Bean Chicken Chili Soup, accompanied by crunchy toast points and Mother's attention. It was truly (a healing) chicken soup for the tailbone.

White Bean Chicken Chili Soup

Ingredients:

2	cups great northern white beans
10	cups low fat chicken stock, divided
5	chicken breast halves, cubed
1	medium yellow onion, chopped
4	cloves garlic, minced
3	tablespoons olive oil
1	can (4-ounce) mild green chilies, chopped
1-1/2	teaspoons cumin
2	teaspoons oregano
1/4	teaspoon pepper
1	bottle (12-ounce) light beer
2-1/2	cups Monterey jack cheese, shredded
	Salt and pepper to taste

Garnish options:

1	cup nonfat plain yogurt
1	cup sour cream
1/2	cup fresh cilantro, chopped
1	cup salsa
1/2	cup Monterey jack cheese, shredded

◈ Cover and soak beans in water overnight in a medium bowl. The next day, cook the chicken in 2 cups of chicken stock in a saucepan until meat is completely cooked through, about 20 to 25 minutes. Set aside. In a large soup pot, sauté onion and garlic in oil for 10 minutes. Add chilies and spices and stir together. Add beans and remainder of chicken stock (8 cups). Bring to a boil. Cover, reduce heat and simmer for 3 hours.

◈ Twenty minutes before serving, add chicken, beer and 2-1/2 cups cheese and simmer. Serve with garnish options.

◈ Serves 8 to 10.

Ingredients:

2	large onions, chopped
5	cloves garlic, minced
2	large red bell peppers, chopped
3	cups fresh tomatoes, chopped and peeled
1	can (35-ounce) tomato puree
3	tablespoons chili powder (for a less spicy chili, use less chili powder)
1	tablespoon dried basil
1	tablespoon dried oregano
1	tablespoon black pepper
1	tablespoon cumin
2	teaspoons salt
2	teaspoons fennel seeds
1/4	cup fresh Italian parsley, chopped
1	can (15-ounce) dark red kidney beans, drained
1	can (15-ounce) garbanzo beans, drained
1	can (15-ounce) black beans, drained
1	can (15-ounce) corn, drained
1/2	cup fresh dill, chopped
1	tablespoon lemon juice
1	tablespoon coriander

Nearly Nonfat Veggie Chili

❀ Cook everything together (except garnish items) in a large sauce or soup pan on medium heat for 10 minutes. Stir. Turn to low and cook covered for 2 hours. Stir occasionally. Serve with garnish options.

❀ Serves 10.

❀ Garnish options:
  - 1 cup nonfat plain yogurt
  - 1 cup cheddar or Monterey jack cheese, grated
  - 1/2 cup scallions, chopped
  - 1 bag tortilla chips
  - 1 cup fresh salsa

Artichoke Leek Soup

Ingredients:

4	leeks, sliced (white part only)
3	tablespoons olive oil
2	cloves garlic, minced
2	baking potatoes, peeled and diced
3	tablespoons rice
1	can (14-ounce) artichoke hearts in water
6	cups chicken broth
1	teaspoon cumin
1/2	teaspoon thyme
1/2	teaspoon cayenne
2	teaspoons pepper
1	tablespoon lemon juice

Garnish:

chives
croutons
sour cream

❀ In a large saucepan or soup pot on medium-high heat, sauté leeks and garlic in olive oil for 5 minutes. Add potatoes, rice, artichoke hearts, chicken broth and spices. Sauté for 5 minutes. Turn heat down and simmer for 45 minutes. Blend portion of soup in blender or food processor on medium speed until fairly smooth and place in large bowl. Repeat until all soup has been blended. Return to saucepan. Stir in lemon juice. Add garnish items to individual servings.

❀ Serves 4 to 6.

Ingredients:

1/2	stick butter, divided
30	cloves garlic
8	cups fish stock, divided
3	baking potatoes, peeled and chopped into small chunks
1	medium white onion, chopped
2	leeks, chopped
1/8	teaspoon salt
2	stalks celery, chopped
2	cups white wine
1	tablespoon white pepper
1	pound scallops
	juice from 1 lemon
1-1/2	cups whipping cream

Garnish options:
    cayenne pepper (easy!)
    chives
    parsley

Roasted Garlic and Scallop Soup

❂ In a stockpot, sauté garlic in 1 tablespoon butter for 2 minutes. Cover with 2 cups fish stock, heat on medium heat until mixture almost boils. Reduce heat to low and cook garlic for 15 minutes. Add potatoes and 3 cups stock, cook until potatoes are soft, about 20 minutes. Melt remaining butter in a skillet, add onions and leeks, sprinkle with salt. Sauté until translucent. Add celery, wine and white pepper. Pour into stock pot with potatoes and garlic and cook for 10 minutes. Puree mixture in blender until smooth, return to pan, increase heat and add remaining fish stock. Add scallops just before serving, cook for 3 minutes — NO MORE. Add lemon juice and whisk in cream. Do not boil soup or it will separate. Garnish bowls with cayenne, chives or parsley.

❂ Serves 8 to 10.

Stick 'Em Up!

The house was quiet while Beth assembled the ingredients for a batch of her friend Laura's famous minestrone soup. She was preparing her family's favorite dinner to be ready and waiting when they returned from a camping weekend. She rarely had the house to herself and had opted to stay home, fully appreciating the sweet sound of silence and an opportunity to do whatever — no plans, no schedules.

Beth loved to cook, and making soup was especially satisfying for her. There was something almost therapeutic about chopping, dicing and stirring what promised to be a hearty soup. Beth was wearing her favorite T-shirt, white cotton undies, and a disreputable pair of pink fuzzy slippers that had seen better days. Her face was covered with a mud mask to cleanse her overworked pores, and she had purple sponge curlers in her hair. All of this gave her the kind of looks that qualified her for a role in *Star Wars Three*.

With the soup slowly baking, Beth sat down with a book while the mud mask and curlers did their job. Through the open screen-door came the sounds of chirping birds and the soft swish of the sprinkler watering the back lawn.

Curled up in a corner of the comfortable couch in the family room, her book cradled in her lap, Beth slowly sipped a glass of Pinot Noir until she decided it was time to change the hose and water the side yard. Looking like a refugee from a second-rate health spa, she went outside followed by the family dog, a black Labrador, to move the sprinklers. The job completed, Beth turned back to the house and watched in frozen horror as her dog pushed the back door shut with her wet black snout.

Knowing full well that the door had automatically locked shut, she ran to check. The door was locked tightly. No need to try the front or patio doors; she had locked them herself earlier. Cold reality dawned: she might have to spend the evening outdoors in her undies and curlers, not to mention a mud-caked face.

Then she remembered that she had given the Bairs, her next-door neighbors, an extra key to her house in case of an emergency. After knocking on her friends' back door without getting a response, Beth turned the doorknob and the unlocked door opened. She tiptoed into the back hall, calling out as she emerged in the family room that flowed into the kitchen; there was no one at home.

First things first. The unpleasant mud pack had to go. Every time Beth took a breath, the dry mud mask cracked, and her face ached with the weight of the so-called beauty treatment. Rummaging around in her neighbors' kitchen drawers, she found a towel, turned on the faucet over the sink, and proceeded to wash the mud off her face.

Bent over the sink with warm water running over her face and slowly dissolving the mud pack, Beth turned ice cold when she felt a heavy object poking in her back, and a heard male voice demanding, "Don't move, or I'll shoot!"

Beth froze to the sink, while brackish brown water ran down her face and hands. Nobody had to tell her not to move — she wasn't able to move. She was paralyzed with fear.

"Turn off the water, keep your hands in sight, and turn around slowly," the voice commanded. It sounded like a scene out of *N.Y.P.D. Blue*, she thought wildly, and prayed silently the voice would turn out to be a cop.

With a shaking hand, she reached for the faucet, turned around in slow motion with brownish goop dripping off her face onto her T-shirt, and came face to face with a pleasant-looking young man holding a remote control in his hand that belonged to some television set. The stranger had a grin on his face as he explained to a shaking Beth that his name was Don, and that he was house-sitting while his friends the Bairs were attending an out-of-town workshop for a few days. He glanced at Beth's brief attire, then took in the rest of her strange get-up, and his grin changed into a healthy burst of laughter.

"I live next door, and got locked out of my house," Beth managed to say, and hurriedly explained her dilemma, pointing out that a key to her place was somewhere in her neighbors' kitchen. All the time she kept wiping her face with the kitchen towel before the mud could dry again.

The whole scene looked too ridiculous to be anything but true, and with the help of Don, Beth located the key to safety. Clutching the soiled towel in one hand, her spare key in the other, she crept out of the house and climbed the fence that separated the two houses in the back, praying fervently that it would be the end of this embarrassing affair. She knew that one day she would be able to laugh at it, but at the moment, that day seemed far off in a nebulous future.

Never had she felt more grateful upon entering her own house. Back in the comfort of her family room, and with a deep sigh, she plopped on the couch, reached for the remnants of her wine, and collapsed. Before the soup was done, she made a vow never to venture outside the friendly walls of her home without wearing enough clothes, or with curlers on her head or mud on her face. "What price, wisdom!"

Laura's Baked Minestrone

Ingredients:

2	tablespoons olive oil
3	pounds beef, cubed
2	medium yellow onions, chopped
4	cloves garlic, chopped
1	teaspoon black pepper
2	tablespoons Italian seasoning
3	cans Campbell's beef broth
3	cans Swanson's beef broth
4	soup cans water
1	can (15-ounce) kidney beans, drained
3	cups carrots, chopped
2	cans (28-ounce) tomatoes
4	cups zucchini, chopped
1	can (8- to 10-ounce) whole black olives, undrained
2-1/2	cups baby shell pasta
1/2	cup Parmesan cheese for garnish

❀ Remove upper rack from oven. Preheat oven to 325 degrees.

❀ In heavy skillet brown beef in olive oil over medium high heat, about 15 to 20 minutes. Add onion, garlic, pepper and seasoning and sauté for 15 to 20 minutes. Remove from heat and place contents into a very large baking pan or roasting pot. Add beef broth and water. Bake covered on lower rack in oven for 1-1/2 hours. Add beans, carrots, tomatoes and bake for another 30 to 40 minutes. Add zucchini, olives, and pasta. Bake for another 40 minutes. When ready to serve, sprinkle spoonfuls of Parmesan cheese on top of individual servings.

❀ Serves 8 to 10.

Ingredients:

2	cups dried white beans
12	slices bacon
1	large yellow onion, chopped
1-1/2	cups mushrooms, sliced
46	ounces chicken broth
2	bay leaves
1	teaspoon white pepper
1	carrot, peeled and chopped
3	tablespoons flour
6	tablespoons cold water

Beth's Bean with Bacon Soup

✾ Soak beans in water to cover overnight. In heavy skillet, fry bacon. Remove to paper towel and pour off drippings, leaving 2 tablespoons. Use fat to sauté onion and mushrooms for 7 minutes. Into stockpot or large saucepan, pour chicken broth, beans, bacon, onion and mushroom mixture, bay leaves, white pepper and carrot and simmer for 2 hours. To thicken soup just before serving, whisk flour and cold water together in a small bowl. Add to soup while simmering; stir well.

✾ Serves 4 to 6.

Sassy Side Dishes

*"Celebrate the happiness that
friends are always giving,
make every day a holiday
and celebrate the living."*

Amanda Bradley

Three-Ring Turkey Circus

Fall was in the air. My friends and I were fresh out of college and — surprise, surprise! — gainfully employed. We all were doing real work at real jobs. The world was ours; we were young, we knew it all and owned it all. What with the turning of the leaves and Thanksgiving around the corner, my domestic urges rose to the surface and I decided to cook my first turkey dinner. After all, there is a first for everything. I loved to cook, and I wanted to get the hang of entertaining. What better time to put practice to action than a holiday.

My guest list grew uncontrolled like weeds in sunshine, and was as varied as the menu. My out-of-hand array of guests consisted of several airplane mechanics, visitors from London, Australia and Africa, childhood chums, college friends, and a few strays and who-knows-whose pals. My mother insisted on helping to make my tiny, slightly mildew-scented apartment a bit more inviting for my first gathering, and brought card tables, linens, flowers, and such. She also donated a generous portion of her delicious stuffing.

First mistake, and first lesson learned: Don't plan a first-anything dinner on a workday. I prepared my turkey on my lunch break, and dashed back and forth between office and house a number of times during brief but noticeable absences from my desk.

A brief tip: Make sure you allow enough time to cook a turkey so your guests can eat dinner before dessert. Timing is almost everything, I learned. When my guests arrived, the tables were set and candles were placed in an attempt to create an inviting, homey atmosphere. I prayed the smoke alarm would not go off and ruin what promised to be a harmonious and even (a bit) elegant evening. Each guest brought a favorite side dish — squash, sweet potatoes, mashed potatoes, green beans, pumpkin pie, even warm beer and a few bottles of wine. It would be quite a feast.

Disaster struck as one of my girlfriends, who had actually cooked a turkey before, checked the beautifully browning bird and announced it was far from ready. It would take a couple of hours more to be done; she spoke with authority.

More drinks were poured. But then, much to my dismay, I found I had forgotten to stir the gravy and ended up with a lumpy mess. Holding back a few tears, gritting my teeth, I snuck out, jumped in my car, went to an all night grocery store to buy a package of gravy mix, tore back and started all over again. I have since learned to not let lumpy gravy spoil any occasion. I just toss it in the blender, or use a hand blender, and the lumps disappear at once.

About ten o'clock in the evening my motley crew finally sat down to dinner. The conversation was lively though a bit beer-warmed and wine-stained. I surprised myself when I realized the meal was delicious. To the great dismay of one of the guests, a South African dinner partner commented on how strange the sweet potatoes tasted. Rather loudly, he said, "Sweet potatoes! These are the farthest thing from sweet potatoes I've ever tasted!"

My friend Celia, an excellent cook, addressed the young man rather sternly. Her nerves were a bit taut, what with her present and past boyfriends in the same room (the past one had appeared uninvited, all the way from London). Celia defended the side dish she had prepared. "These are not sweet potatoes, you nitwit! This is my mother's third-generation recipe for baked squash!" The South African grinned something between a compliment and an apology, had a second helping, and equanimity was established quickly.

Aside from the powdered gravy, a few mild insults, ex-boyfriends, new boyfriends, and starving friends, the evening turned out very well, and preparing a turkey dinner each year for a gathering of friends became a tradition. Turkey Circus turned into an annual event.

Ingredients:

3	cups sweet potatoes
1/2	teaspoon salt
1/2	cup milk
1	teaspoon vanilla
1	cup sugar
2	eggs
3	tablespoons butter
1	teaspoon cinnamon

Topping:
1	cup brown sugar
1/3	cup flour
3	tablespoons butter, softened
1	cup nuts, chopped

Sweet Potato Casserole

❀ Preheat oven to 350 degrees.

❀ When using fresh potatoes, boil in their skins until tender to the fork, drain well, peel and mash. When using canned sweet potatoes, drain well and mash. Add remaining ingredients except topping and mix well. Turn into an 8 x 8 x 2 inch lightly greased casserole dish.

❀ Mix topping ingredients together, pour on top of potato mixture. Bake for 35 minutes.

❀ Serves 6.

Ingredients:

8	handfuls fresh green beans
2	quarts water
6	sprigs fresh rosemary (leave one for garnish)
1	cup balsamic vinegar
1	cup olive oil
1	tablespoon black pepper
2	tablespoons basil
2	tablespoons oregano
2	tablespoons thyme
1	tablespoon sugar
6	cloves garlic, minced
1/2	cup pinenuts, toasted

Marinated Green Beans

❀ Rinse beans, cut off stem ends. In a large saucepan bring 2 quarts of water to boiling. Add beans, boil about 4 minutes; drain. Place beans in a 9 x 13 inch baking dish. Mix vinegar, olive oil, herbs, spices, sugar and garlic together. Pour over beans; marinate overnight in refrigerator. Toss beans thoroughly to evenly distribute dressing a couple of times while marinating. Bring to room temperature before serving; drain dressing, add pinenuts. Place on platter and add sprig of rosemary on top of beans for garnish.

❀ Serves 8.

Ingredients:

1	medium eggplant, cut into 2-inch chunks
2	medium zucchini, cut into 2-inch chunks
3	yellow squash, cut into 2-inch chunks
2	medium red peppers, cut into 2-inch chunks
12	small mushrooms
3/4	cup olive oil
1/4	cup balsamic vinegar
1	teaspoon salt
1/4	teaspoon pepper
1	clove garlic, minced
1	tablespoons fresh basil, chopped
1	tablespoon fresh oregano, chopped
1	tablespoon fresh parsley chopped
6	barbeque skewers

Grilled Vegetables

❀ Place vegetables in a medium bowl. In a small bowl, stir together oil, vinegar, salt, pepper, garlic and herbs. Drizzle vinaigrette over vegetables, stirring to coat. Keep at room temperature for 30 minutes. Skewer vegetable pieces.
Barbeque or broil in oven for 8 to 12 minutes or until tender inside and golden brown outside.

❀ Serves 6.

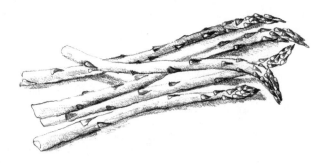

Carrot Mousse

Ingredients:

4	cups carrots, peeled, cut into 1-inch pieces (about 1 full 32-ounce bag of carrots)
4	tablespoons butter
1/2	cup cream
2	eggs
1/4	teaspoon salt
1/4	teaspoon pepper

❋ Preheat oven to 350 degrees.

❋ In a saucepan cover carrots with water and cook until tender, about 20 to 25 minutes. Drain; add rest of ingredients and puree until very, very smooth in food processor. Turn mousse into baking casserole dish, set in water bath and bake in oven for 1-1/4 hours.

❋ Serves 4 to 6.

❋ Note: For water bath use a shallow pan, 2 inches deep but large enough to hold casserole. Fill half-full with hot water and place casserole dish with carrots in pan.

Good to the Last Dip

Joy and Cindy were a great help assisting me in researching and testing recipes for this cookbook. Next on the list was one of my friends' famous barbeque sauce, and we decided to get together for a Sunday afternoon barbeque. The sauce was on trial and the *raison d'etre*.

While the men were doing their barbeque routine on the patio, and catching up on each other's business, my girlfriends and I gathered in the kitchen chatting and chopping. According to directions, the sauce was to simmer long enough to "reduce liquid to half."

During the simmering period, we did a lot of taste-and-test bread-dipping which was our way of "reducing" the liquid. We were not alone. One by one the boys kept trotting into the kitchen to see what was keeping the barbeque sauce from getting done so they could start grilling the meat. They also tasted and tested and dipped into the delicious sauce — a lot!

Well, the sauce was dip-tested one too many times, and there wasn't enough left to coat a cocktail wiener. The evening was turning into night, and we still hadn't started grilling the main course. After all the work and time we had invested to produce an extraordinary barbeque meal, I had to do a most ordinary thing. I rushed out to the nearest grocery store and grabbed the first bottle of barbeque sauce from the shelf. It had to do.

The next time I made the sauce, I doubled the recipe in preparation for dipping, tasting and testing, and was thrilled to have enough sauce to baste the chicken and a few ribs.

Barbeque Sauce

Ingredients:

2	tablespoons butter
1	medium onion, finely chopped
2	tablespoons vinegar
1/4	cup lemon juice
2	tablespoons brown sugar
1/8	teaspoon cayenne pepper
1	cup catsup
1	tablespoon dry mustard
1	cup water
1/2	cup celery, chopped

❀ In a saucepan simmer all ingredients for 25 to 35 minutes. Stir occasionally as sauce gets quite thick.

❀ Use to baste spareribs, chicken or favorite meat to grill on barbeque.

Nearer My God to Thee

Linda and Charlie Hall were not only Megan and Robert Brown's neighbors, but the foursome considered themselves best friends. It was as natural as falling off a log when the Browns decided to celebrate Linda's thirtieth birthday with a small dinner party. Both their children were spending the weekend with cousins, which gave Megan time to prepare a more detailed dinner. She added another course to the menu and did handstands with the dessert.

Megan invited another couple, fussed with flowers and candles, and the evening turned out well. Champagne and conversation bubbled along nicely. The cornish game hens, roasted to golden perfection, and Linda's favorite side dish, a green chile soufflé, didn't have a chance of becoming leftovers. Shortly after the other guests had said their goodbyes around midnight, Linda and husband Charlie got into an argument over nothing more serious than a butterfly's hiccup.

While Megan and Robert sat by helplessly, their friends' difference of opinions escalated into a full-fledged shouting match and Charlie, furious, grabbed his wife's purse with the car keys and tore out of the house, slamming the door behind him so hard a picture fell off the wall. He roared down Johnson Road, and everyone could hear the squealing of wheels on the gravel when Charlie turned into his driveway, less than five hundred feet from his hosts' house.

After some more champagne, lots of hand-holding and soothing talk, Robert and Megan walked a subdued Linda home in the crisp air of the early fall night. Johnson Road consisted of widely-spaced homes which sat on one or more acres. Tall cottonwoods and hedge-lined fences provided the residents with privacy in a serene country-like setting at the edge of suburbia. It was a most unique and pleasant street that ran for almost one mile without interruptions of side streets dissecting its flow.

When the three friends arrived at Linda's front door, they found it locked securely, and there was no response to the steady pounding of three sets of fists.

Surely, there were more ways than one to get into a house. The little group walked around to the back only to find the patio door locked as well. They finally grabbed handfuls of green apples from under the crippled old apple tree and fired them rapidly at the upstairs windows of the master suite. A window flew open. Charlie, known for his hair-raising pranks, stuck his head out into the night, and true to form, he sternly said, "Go away. I don't know you. I don't know any of you!" With that he disappeared from sight, and left his wife standing in the garden.

Linda refused the invitation to spend the rest of the night in her friends' guest room. She was certain Charlie had sent the sitter home, and she needed to be at the house with the couple's three children.

A brilliant idea crossed Robert's mind. "We have a big ladder at the house that the roofers left behind. Let's get it," he suggested, overcome with the sheer genius of his plan. "It'll reach to the second floor, Linda, and you can climb into your bedroom."

Whether his plan was reasonable, or whether the champagne enhanced their sense of adventure, the trio toddled back down Johnson Road to the Browns' house and from the side of the garage, they retrieved the heavy, tall ladder belonging to the the workmen. Robert took the lead, Linda grabbed the middle and Megan brought up the rear. Dressed to kill, the women wearing three-inch heels, strings of pearls and ankle-length gowns, and Robert decked out in dark pinstripes and silk tie, they must have made quite a picture strutting down the road at four o'clock on a Sunday morning carrying a ladder fit for a roofer.

A car approached, slowed down and stopped. The driver rolled down his window, stuck out head, looked the gang over and asked, "Where in the hell are you going with that ladder?" Obviously the man had seen too many *Mission Impossible* shows.

Living just around the corner from a large Catholic church came in handy. Robert, without missing a step, flung back his head. "It's nearer my God to Thee, my good man, and we've just attended extra-early mass," he shouted with conviction, as he turned into Linda's driveway. The man shook his head, digesting what he had heard and seen, sat for another moment leaning out of the car window, and finally went on his way.

With the ladder leaning securely against the house, high heels and all, Linda gingerly climbed rung after rung with Robert and Megan holding on. Before Linda even reached the window sill, Charlie appeared at the bedroom window, waving his arms wildly about as though conducting a runaway orchestra. "If you don't go away," he shrieked in a stage-like falsetto voice with southern overtones, "I'll call the police and report a break-in in progress." With that he slammed the window shut.

Linda kept pounding on the small glass panes, as her friends steadied the ladder — surely, Charlie had had his fun and would let his wife into the house. In less than three minutes a police car with flashing red lights screeched to a halt at the end of the long driveway. Two cops popped out of the black and white vehicle and raced around the house to the back yard, guns drawn.

Charlie reappeared, sticking his head out of another second-floor window, shouting, "Take them away, officer, I don't know these people."

Something in the trio's get-up and their fast talk must have convinced the policemen that a practical joker might be at work. The officers, sternly, in their best no-nonsense, we're-de-law voices, directed Charlie to open the door. Finally, a pajama-clad Charlie appeared. His usual ear-to-ear prankster grin was gone. His face was set in his version of injured dignity. Briskly, the officers established Linda's marital status, reprimanded the prankster, called the scene a "domestic incident," cited him for being a public nuisance, and left.

Clutching the summons in his hand in disbelief of a good thing gone wrong, Charles Hall followed Linda into the house, she most probably preparing herself for Act Two of the next go-around.

With visions of polishing off the remains of a lovely dinner in his head as soon as he got home, Robert grabbed the lead end of the heavy ladder. Megan reached for the other end, and singing "Nearer My God To Thee" — making up lyrics to fit the occasion — the pair trotted down Johnson Road to their house.

Robert was dreaming of leftover game hens, cold but delicious, multiple side dishes, and dessert, but Megan just thought about sleep.

With the monster ladder leaning safely against the back of the garage, the adventure had come to an end, or so they thought. The front door wouldn't budge; neither did the back door. Megan and Robert had locked themselves out of the house.

Baked Beans

Ingredients:

1	pound lean ground beef
1/2	white onion, chopped
8	slices bacon
3/4	cup brown sugar
2	tablespoons vinegar
1/2	cup catsup
1	teaspoon salt
2	tablespoons prepared Dijon mustard
1	can (15-ounce) lima beans, drained
1	can (15-ounce) baked beans, drained
1	can (15-ounce) kidney beans, drained
1	can (15-ounce) black-eyed peas, drained
1	can (15-ounce) pinto beans, drained

❀ In a heavy saucepan, brown ground beef with onion for about 10 to 12 minutes; drain excess grease. In a skillet, cut raw bacon into bits, brown and drain. Add bacon to ground beef and onion; add sugar, vinegar, catsup, salt and mustard, stir well. Add all beans. Simmer on medium heat for 30 to 45 minutes. Stir occasionally.

❀ Serves 8.

Sheila's Baked Rice

Ingredients:

3   cups sour cream
2   cans (4-ounces each) mild
       chopped green chilies
5   cups cooked rice
2   medium zucchini, thinly sliced
4   medium tomatoes, chopped
2-1/2 cups Monterey jack cheese,
       shredded
2-1/2 cups cheddar cheese, shredded

❀   Heat oven to 350 degrees.
❀   Mix sour cream with chopped chilies. In a 2-quart casserole dish place one-third of rice, layer half of sliced zucchini, next layer half of tomatoes. Spread half of sour cream mixture and then half of Monterey jack cheese. Repeat layers. Finish by topping with rice. Bake for 50 to 60 minutes. Top with cheddar cheese. Bake for 10 more minutes.
❀   Serves 8.

Sue's Spicy Noodles

Ingredients:

1/2	cup soy sauce
1/2	cup sesame oil
1/4	cup sugar
1/4	cup rice wine vinegar
1	tablespoon hot pepper oil (add 1 tablespoon more if you like it)
1	pound vermicelli pasta, cooked and drained, not rinsed
1/4	cup sesame seeds, toasted
1/4	cup green onions, chopped

❀ Mix first 5 ingredients, add hot noodles. Keep at room temperature, stirring occasionally. Just before serving add sesame seeds and green onions.

❀ Serves 6.

Potatoes Gone Chic

Good, old-fashioned butter-and-milk whipped potatoes have gone "nouvelle." Hardly a gourmet magazine issue goes by that doesn't come up with one more version of "designer mashed potatoes." Everything from rutabaga to garlic, to carrots, turnips, celery bottoms and crushed walnuts has been added to the whipping process for the more than patient American mashed potato. There are some recipes for the once lowly spud, so strange that they defy description, knocking about the gourmet circles. But here's one that's safe and delicious.

Garlic – Cream Cheese Mashed Potatoes

Ingredients:

2	tablespoons olive oil
2	whole heads garlic
5	pounds Golden or russet potatoes
1	package (8-ounce) light cream cheese
3/4	cup low-fat chicken broth
1/4	teaspoon salt
1/4	teaspoon white pepper

❀ Preheat oven to 375 degrees.

❀ Cut heads of garlic in half and place cut side down in olive oil on cookie sheet. Bake uncovered for 35 minutes, or until bottoms of garlic heads are light brown. Remove from oven and press garlic from skin. Reserve. Leave oven on for cooking potatoes.

❀ While garlic is cooking, peel potatoes and cut into 2-inch chunks. Boil until soft, about 30 minutes. Hand-mash potatoes, adding cream cheese, chicken broth and garlic. Season with salt and white pepper. Place mixture in a 2-1/2 quart casserole dish. Bake for about 30 minutes.

❀ Serves 8.

❀ Can be prepared a day ahead.

Pilfered Pasta

"We may live without poetry, music, and art;
We may live without conscience,
*   and live without heart;*
We may live without friends;
*   we may live without books;*
But civilized man can not live without Cooks."
                    Edward Robert Bulwer-Lytton

Whatever Happened to Plain Spaghetti?

What kind of a world was it before the Italians took over the kitchens of America? More popular than French cuisine, simpler than German meals, and less exotic than Asian dishes, pasta is everybody's taste.

And, pasta has come a long way. It may have started when a batch of "Jewish" noodles from the north coast of Africa crossed the Mediterranean, landed in an Italian household, were transformed, and emerged as spaghetti from a kitchen in Napoli. After that, there was no stopping the shapes the simple egg-water-and-flour dough took on. From alphabet to linguini, to orzo, to vermicilli, to ziti — tossed with oil, smothered with tomatoes, sauced, peppered with fungi and served with fish and fowl, pasta has become the chosen favorite everywhere.

Just as lively, spicy and satisfying as a pasta meal is the Italian kitchen that produces all that wonderful Mediterranean soul food. This is the place where generations meet, teach, chat and cook. With a tantalizing marinara softly bubbling on the stove and fragrant biscotti baking in the oven, a grandmother, between thumb and forefinger, pinches gnocchi into shape. With admirable precision, look-alike ravioli filled with a fragrant cheese mixture appear from the hands of her daughter, while the young girls chop, mince and peel vegetables and greens. Talk mingles with laughter, older voices teach and scold, an occasional flash of Italian temper raises the temperature in the family kitchen, as three generations under one roof prepare the evening meal.

Whether it is village gossip in one kitchen, or a heated debate in another, Italians not only know how to cook, they know how make it a family affair — may the tradition live on.

Zesty Ziti

Ingredients:

1	pound ziti pasta, cooked al dente (follow package instructions)
2	tablespoons olive oil
2	cloves garlic, minced
1	small yellow onion, chopped
2	cups prepared tomato sauce
1	teaspoon dried basil
16	ounces ricotta cheese
1	cup Parmesan cheese, freshly grated, divided
1	egg white
1/4	teaspoon salt
1/2	teaspoon pepper
1-1/4	cups mozzarella cheese, shredded

❀ Preheat oven to 350 degrees.

❀ Sauté garlic and onions in olive oil for 10 minutes. Mix in tomato sauce. Add basil, set aside. In a small bowl combine ricotta, 3/4 cup Parmesan, egg white, salt and pepper. Set aside.

❀ Combine cooked ziti with ricotta mixture, mozzarella and 1-1/2 cups of tomato sauce. In a 2-quart casserole dish, spread 1/4 cup tomato sauce on the bottom, add pasta mixture. Cover with remaining 1/4 cup tomato sauce. Sprinkle 1/4 cup Parmesan cheese on top, cover and bake for 35 to 40 minutes or until heated through.

❀ Serves 6 to 8.

Lulu's Crawfish Fettuccine

Lulu, a southern siren from Shreveport, opened her restaurant and backroom bootleg bar during the Roaring Twenties. She had retired from a ten-year career as a professional dancer, exchanging her tap shoes for a frying pan. This enterprising woman managed to accumulate a total of nine husbands and five children, all of whom had different fathers. At the time of operating her restaurant, husband number four — or was it five? — helped her run their popular dining establishment. People loved the chummy atmosphere that prevailed in the funky little place, and raved about the food that came from Lulu's kitchen.

She always wore her trademark red, and was known to bellow colorful obscenities whenever her prep-cook Clayton sampled too much of the bootleg liquor. Lulu's Place was a lively spot, where one could pass the time with good friends, engage in lively conversation and enjoy an excellent meal. Lulu often joined her guests at their tables, bought a round of drinks, talked about this and that, and was a good pal to all.

She stayed up late night after night, but was known to rise with the sun, go to her kitchen and fry huge batches of bacon and eggs for those stragglers who were still hanging around from the night before. She loved to cook, and few knew that she preferred cooking in the nude on steamy summer days. A red apron hung from a hook in her tidy kitchen for those special mornings when she fried bacon in the nude, since a slight accident when hot bacon drippings had leapt out of the pan and sizzled her pendulous breasts.

There came the day when Lulu's Place was the jumpingest joint in town, and it all happened in the morning. Looking back on the fateful day, Lulu admits sheepishly, a wide grin splitting her face, that the disaster was bound to happen sooner or later.

It had been an unusually humid August morning when Lulu walked sleepily into her kitchen to cook a late breakfast — early lunch for some of the regulars who hadn't bothered to go home and were a hungry bunch. Stark naked, she slipped on her short, red apron that far from covered her bare beginnings, and left her exposed at the rear and on her sides, not to mention her ample front. She peeked through a crack in the door to see just how many she'd have to feed for breakfast, and proceeded to bang pans and dishes around, frying batches of spicy sausage and peppery bacon. She beat several dozen eggs with her special seasoning to a frothy pale yellow, and skillfully scrambled them until the hens' pride were a fluffy heap of perfection. She set out the dishes, fixed eight plates with eggs, sausage and bacon, and rested a few pieces of fruit next to the fried potatoes.

Still half asleep, she took off her apron, kicked open the swinging door that led straight into the dining room with her bare toes, and stifling a big yawn, proceeded to place the breakfast plates in front of her loyal customers, totally unaware of the strange looks of some her patrons, and seemingly immune to the wild whistles that greeted her from others. Having dispensed with the first serving, she turned her bare bottom on the gang and went back toward the kitchen for the last four plates. She thought the whistling and slapping and clapping and stomping of feet were simply a tribute to her fine breakfast fixings, until she saw herself in a full-length mirror on the way back to her kitchen.

It was quite a sight that greeted her as she stood glued to the floor, unable to move for what seemed an eternity. What would be the most dignified way to escape? If she backed out into the kitchen her front was on display. If she turned, her rear was exposed. With a fiery-red blush spreading on her face, mustering up her most effective who-gives-a-damn attitude, she squared her shoulders, turned her back to her guests and stomped out of the dining room. The second serving had to wait a while; the hostess got dressed.

Men gossip too, and the story of Lulu's topless, backless bareness quickly spread around town, a matter which turned out to be good for business. Men stood in line for breakfast, hoping for a repeat performance of Lulu's appearance *au natural*. Lulu's modest little restaurant filled up with curious men for dinner as well, and she kept right on making her most famous dish — Lulu's Crawfish

Fettuccine.

One of her five children passed this recipe down to her granddaughter Missy, who owns a café in Shreveport named for her amazing great-grandmother. There will always be a Lulu's Place — where a red apron hangs on a hook in the kitchen, ready to "cover" the cook.

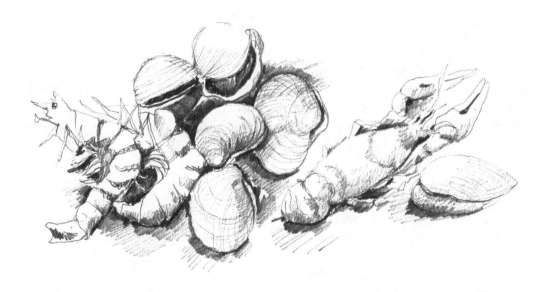

Lulu's Crawfish Fettuccine

Ingredients:

1	pound fettuccine
3/4	teaspoon salt
1/2	teaspoon onion powder
1/2	teaspoon cayenne powder
1/2	teaspoon white pepper
1/2	teaspoon paprika
1/2	teaspoon thyme
1/4	teaspoon black pepper
1	stick butter
1	bunch green onions, chopped
1	clove garlic, minced
1	pound cooked crawfish (cooked shrimp can be substituted)
1/2	cup chicken stock

❀ Combine all spices in small container, set aside. Cook fettuccine. In medium sauce pan, melt butter, sauté chopped green onions and garlic for 5 minutes. Add cooked crawfish, chicken stock; simmer for 5 more minutes. Mix in spices (use to taste — mixture is very spicy). Combine with fettuccine and serve.

❀ Serves 4 to 6.

Black Beans and Angel Hair Pasta

Ingredients:

1	can (15-ounce) black beans, rinsed and drained
1/2	cup canned low fat chicken stock
2	teaspoons Oriental sesame oil
1	teaspoon soy sauce
2	cloves garlic, minced
1/4	teaspoon dried red pepper flakes
1	teaspoon black pepper
1/2	teaspoon salt
1	teaspoon granulated sugar
1/4	teaspoon ground cumin
1/4	teaspoon ground ginger
3/4	cup yellow onion, finely diced kernels from 2 ears of fresh corn (approximately 2/3 cup)
1/2	red pepper, thinly sliced
1	pound angel hair pasta

Garnish options:
peanuts
fresh cilantro
salsa and sour cream
juice of 2 limes

❀ In a medium saucepan, combine beans, chicken stock, sesame oil, soy sauce, garlic, red pepper flakes, black pepper, salt, sugar, cumin, ginger and onion. Simmer on medium heat for 20 minutes, stirring occasionally. Add corn and red pepper slices and cook for 10 more minutes. Meanwhile, cook pasta according to directions until al dente; drain well and toss with black bean mixture. Garnish with peanuts, cilantro, salsa and sour cream. Sprinkle with a little lime juice. Serve hot.

❀ Serves 6 to 8.

Vegetarian Lasagna

Ingredients:

Zucchini Red Sauce:
1/4	cup olive oil
2	cloves garlic, chopped fine
1	medium yellow onion, peeled and chopped
3	cups tomatoes, chopped (fresh or canned)
1/4	cup Italian parsley, chopped
1/2	cup dry red wine
1/2	teaspoon basil
1/2	teaspoon oregano
1/2	teaspoon salt
1/4	teaspoon pepper
2	zucchinis, thinly sliced

Lasagna mixture:
1	package lasagna noodles
3	tablespoons olive oil, divided
12	ounces nonfat cottage cheese
1	egg, beaten
1/4	cup parsley, chopped
1	cup mozzarella cheese, shredded
1/2	cup Parmesan cheese, grated

❀ Zucchini Red Sauce:

❀ Heat olive oil on medium high heat. Sauté garlic and onion until clear, about 10 to 15 minutes. Add tomatoes, parsley, wine and spices. Simmer for about 15 minutes. Add sliced zucchini; simmer until zucchini is tender, about 10 minutes.

❀ Assembling lasagna:

❀ Preheat oven to 375 degrees.

❀ Cook noodles in boiling water with one tablespoon olive oil according to package directions. While noodles are cooking, combine cottage cheese with egg and parsley in small bowl and set aside. Drain noodles. Rub remaining 2 tablespoons olive oil on bottom of lasagna pan. Fill pan with alternate layers of noodles, 1/3 of zucchini tomato sauce, 1/2 cottage cheese mixture, and half mozzarella. Repeat. Top with remaining sauce and Parmesan cheese. Cover pan with foil and bake for 1 hour. Uncover, continue baking for 15 minutes until bubbly and heated through. Let stand for about 10 minutes before serving.

La Dolce Vita

The next best thing to lunching in Umbria, dining in Tuscany, and drinking Italian wine in the rest of the country, is having ingredients available that sing Italian, look Italian and make you dream Italian. With the ever-growing popularity of Italian cuisine, specialty food stores have finally sprung up in suburbs, towns and cities all over America. These wonderful little stores drown in the aroma of ripe hunks of Romano, tender wedges of Bel Paese, and the king of them all, the popular Parmesano. Olive oils — extra virgin and related, vinegars in herb- and vegetable-cluttered bottles, clusters of garlic, imported jars of marinara, dried porcini, families of olives, and a kaleidoscope of pastas bring us the heart and soul of Italian foods, if not the landscape itself.

Fortunately for us Northwesterners, the flavors of Italy have found a welcome home in our part of the country. I know of such a place which I think is strictly there for my convenience, and to satisfy my passion for *la bella Italia*. Kim and Bill Horton made three big changes in their lives several years ago, all of which have agreed with them. They moved to the Pacific Northwest, exchanged wedding vows, and opened Port City Pasta, an Italian grocery in a suburb of Portland. Kim and Bill share a passion for food, wine and people, topped only by their love for anything Italian.

They have combed the shelves of import houses and brought us food and wine — a virtual harvest of culinary goodies from North, Central and sunny Southern Italy — to our slightly soggy land. Talented cooks themselves, the couple prepare their own recipes straight from the best *cucina Italia*. Many is the time I have strayed there and walked home with one of their take-out-*Italiano* meals, a loaf of crisp bread, and a good bottle of wine. When a perfect meal ends with praise for my efforts, I simply smile mysteriously at my family, and quietly mumble a faint, *"Mille, mille grazie."*

Port City Pasta Seafood Lasagna

Ingredients:

1/4	stick butter
1	cup celery, chopped
1	cup yellow onion, chopped
3/4	cup red bell pepper, chopped
1	pound fresh shrimp, rinsed well
1	pound fresh crab meat

White Sauce:

1	pint whole milk
1/2	stick butter
1/4	cup flour
8	ounces sour cream
1	tablespoon butter, melted (for bottom of pan)
3	sheets fresh pasta or 12 lasagna noodles
2	cups mozzarella cheese, shredded
2	cups cheddar cheese, shredded
1	cup Parmesan cheese, grated

❊ Melt butter and sauté celery, onion and red pepper for about 5 minutes. Add crab and shrimp, sauté for three more minutes; set aside.

❊ White sauce:
❊ Heat milk in saucepan over medium-low heat. Melt butter on low in a separate saucepan, add flour, cook for 2 to 3 minutes while whisking continuously. Add scalded milk a little at a time; fold in sour cream. Stir together, heat and cook at low boil for about 3 minutes. Set aside.

❊ Assembling lasagna:
❊ Preheat oven to 350 degrees.
❊ Butter bottom of 9 x 12 inch baking dish. Start with layer of pasta, spread half of white sauce, cover with half of seafood mixture, 1 cup mozzarella cheese, 1 cup cheddar cheese, and 1/2 cup Parmesan cheese. Repeat layers. Bake for 45 to 50 minutes or until bubbly. Let stand about 10 minutes before serving.
❊ Serves 8.

Bringing-Baby-Home Lasagna

Blessed with a fertile imagination, Alexandra tackled life with gusto, wild theories and a penchant for the extra-out-of-the-ordinary. She was rarely chagrined by her self-inflicted disasters and gone-the-other-way adventures. That's life, she explained, and insisted that a good laugh healed the soul and wiped clean the slate of guilt and other low-life feelings. Being able to laugh at one's self, she insisted, promoted self-forgiveness. The time would come when Alexandra needed a double dose of her own medicine.

Barely twenty years old, she had her first baby, a sturdy little boy she named Alexander (the Little). Early in her pregnancy, she had voiced her concern to her physician that perhaps motherhood was not her strong suit, and expressed her hope that the good doctor would be able able to deliver a healthy dose of the same along with the new baby. Assured by the man who would help bring her baby into the world that motherhood was the most natural thing, she felt she'd have as good a chance as the next woman to be a fine mother.

When the baby was two weeks old, Alexandra had to take him for his two-week checkup, and also needed to discuss a postpartum problem at the same visit. Getting to town would take at least forty minutes, and adding the waiting around at the doctor's office, Alexandra knew the outing would take the better part of the day. She had fixed a lasagna early in the morning, so the evening meal would be be ready and waiting.

Her mother Lucy wanted to go along, offering to pay the expenses for the long taxi ride to the city. The family had immigrated to the United States two years earlier, and although everyone was working, they did not own an automobile. That would come later. Taking a cab was quite a luxury, but seemed a better solution than the slow ride on the streetcar that hot summer day.

When the cab driver deposited his passengers at the doctor's downtown office, Alexandra told him that if he wished to hire on for the return trip, he would need to be back at the doctor's office within the hour. The friendly man nodded, pleased with the opportunity to have a paying fare back to his territory.

A German refugee like them, Albert Weil was not only their doctor but had befriended the family, and theirs had developed into a comfortable and pleasant social relationship. Dr. Weil checked the baby, eased Alexandra's concerns, made his recommendations, chatted about this, that and the other, and handed her several prescription slips, and the friends parted. When Alexandra appeared in the doctor's outer office where her mother was waiting, she didn't notice her mother's puzzled expression, and to the older woman's question, "Do you have everything?" Alexandra checked her purse, the handful of prescriptions and the sample pills, nodded and led the way out of the doctor's office.

Back on the street, like clockwork, the nice cab driver was waiting. He revved his motor and took off for home. After they had gone a block or two in comfortable silence, he stopped at a red light, turned around to face his passengers, and in a concerned voice said, "It's too bad your little boy is so sick you had to leave him at the doctor's."

Alexandra turned green, then red-hot, grabbed her flat tummy, checked her empty arms and looked at her mother, whose brown eyes reflected her thoughts. "Oh, my God," Alexandra howled, " I left him at the doctor's! Turn around, please. I left my baby at the doctor's!"

A wide conspiratory grin crossed the driver's face as he wheeled the car around and just a few moments later pulled up in front of the granite-faced office building. Tucked against the heavy oak door in a corner of the huge entryway, out of the glare and heat of the sun, stood one of Doctor Weil's nurses cradling a white flannel-wrapped bundle. Alexandra shot out of the car, and held out her arms, babbling something or other, her face as red as a ripe tomato. The nurse laughed softly, saying that everyone had bet it wouldn't take long for even a new mother like Alexandra to discover that she carried her baby on the outside from now on.

Nothing had ever felt better in her life than cradling that baby in her arms. She reentered the cab and shot an accusing glance at her mother. "Why did you let me walk out without the baby?" she demanded.

Lucy's eyes softened, and a smile spread over her face as she reached for her daughter's hand and said, "How else will you learn your responsibilities? How will you learn to play the role of mother if I write the script for you?"

Alexandra let the message sink in for a second, started to chuckle under her breath, kissed her son soundly on his downy-soft cheeks, and true to her nature, let laughter boil out of her healing soul, as she vowed never, ever to let her child down.

Bringing-Baby-Home Lasagna

Ingredients:

1	pound extra lean ground beef (or turkey)
3/4	cup low fat chicken broth
32	ounces prepared marinara sauce
8	ounces uncooked lasagna noodles
1-1/2	cups low fat cottage cheese, divided
2	cups mozzarella cheese, shredded, divided
3/4	cup Parmesan cheese, grated, divided

❀ Preheat oven to 375 degrees.
❀ Brown ground beef in non-stick skillet and drain off juices. Add chicken stock and marinara sauce. In a 9 X 13 inch glass baking dish, layer sauce, uncooked lasagna noodles, cottage cheese, mozzarella cheese; repeat layers, ending with sauce and Parmesan cheese. Cover dish with foil and bake for 50 minutes. Remove foil, bake for an additional 10 minutes. Let stand 15 minutes before cutting into squares.
❀ Serves 6 to 8.

Cathy's Pinenut Pesto Sauce

Ingredients:

3	cups fresh basil
1/2	cup olive oil
4	cloves garlic
1/4	teaspoon salt
1/4	cup pine nuts
1/4	cup Parmesan cheese

❀ In a blender or food processor, combine all ingredients. Blend until all is chopped fine.

❀ Makes about 1-1/4 cups fresh pesto sauce.

Cindy's Hazelnut Pesto Sauce

Ingredients:

2   cups fresh basil leaves
1/2   cup olive oil
1/3   cup Romano cheese, grated
1/3   cup Parmesan cheese, grated
1/4   cup hazelnuts (filberts)
2   cloves garlic, minced
1/8   teaspoon salt
1/8   teaspoon pepper

❀   Blend all ingredients in food processor.
❀   Makes about 1 cup.

Pesto Pasta Salad

Ingredients:

1	pound radiatore pasta
1	jar (8-ounce) sundried tomatoes packed in oil
1	cup walnuts, coarsely chopped
1-1/2	cups feta cheese, crumbled
1-1/2	cups Parmesan cheese, shredded
3/4 – 1	cup fresh pesto sauce (see index)
1	teaspoon salt
1	tablespoon black pepper

❋ Cook pasta according to package directions until al dente. Do not overcook! Drain well, do not rinse! Place pasta in a large bowl. Let cool for a few minutes, add all ingredients. Mix thoroughly. Serve at room temperature. If pasta gets dry, add 1/4 cup more pesto sauce or olive oil.

❋ Serves 10.

Embezzled Entrees

*"Food imaginatively and lovingly prepared, and
eaten in good company, warms the being with
something more than the mere intake of calories."*
Marjorie Kinnan Rawlings

Agatha's Black Tie Dinner

Agatha Downey-Blake did not just belong to the inner circle of Belville's society, she was the very top of the upper crust. The small town on the banks of the Great Muddy had become Agatha's home after she married miner-turned-big-time-rancher Vernon Downey-Blake and reluctantly traded Chicago's social scene for the wide open spaces of Big-Sky Montana. She left behind her friends and family, theater and concerts, fine restaurants, charity balls and the rest of a sophisticated city's offerings.

What this vital and beautiful young woman did not leave behind, however, was her mischievous nature and her passion for adventure. She'd just as soon turn a nightingale into a hawk, or a simple country fair into a gala white-tie affair, as attend a meeting of the Ladies of Hope Committee.

Fortunately four babies, one right after the other, kept her busy for several years, but when the children were on their own, so was Agatha. Frequent travels provided the necessary change of scenery for her, and an African safari as well as trips to the far-flung corners of the globe temporarily satisfied her taste for adventure.

She filled the stately home Vernon had built for her with treasures and mementos of her wanderings, perfected her cuisine with the help of old Jossie, and set a table that was the envy of Belville. Agatha's dinner invitations were coveted, not just for the gourmet delights so alien to the wilds of Montana that the perfect hostess created for her guests, but also for the unexpected she managed to conjure up. Her table settings were legendary and ranged from Louis XIV courtly, to down-on-the-ranch homey, to Victorian frilly-lacy, or art deco funny. Her table always sizzled with excitement as did the flow of the conversation. Most often wearing exotic attire and outrageous jewels at her parties, she'd surprise her friends with impromptu poetry readings, predictions from an out-of-town astrologer, the presence of a mystic seer, or the playing of clever parlor games. The

Big Muddy had never met the likes of her. Agatha Downey-Blake expanded the horizons and added adventure to the lives of those fortunate enough to belong to her circle. She was an unforgettable character.

It was a day in early spring when the town buzzed with speculations, as a dozen or so of Belville's elite received Agatha Downey-Blake's invitation to a "Unique and Definitely 'First Ever'" dinner party at Blake House. A lot of white shirts were being starched, dinner jackets brushed, silk gowns freshly steamed, and two of the best local beauty parlors were booked solid within fifteen minutes of the arrival of the creamy linen notes with the well-known gold seal on their envelopes. It would be quite a night, people predicted, as they shivered deliciously with anticipation.

Arriving at Agatha's house, the guests were greeted by waiters in formal attire carrying trays with heavy crystal flutes of champagne. Surrounded by a wreath of fresh greens and small white blossoms, a unique ice carving in the shape of a penguin presided over a hors d'oeuvres table draped to the floor with a black cloth. The icy bird held a generous amount of richly glistening beluga caviar in its open beak, and four handsome crystal bowls in silver filigree fittings contained the accompanying condiments. Delicate pieces of melon wrapped in pale pink prosciutto shared an old Russian silver platter with slices of wine-cured lox nestled against half-moon slices of lemons. What a sumptuous offering. How could Agatha possibly outdo herself at dinner? Guests were munching, chatting and furtively looking around the grand salon for some signs of the "Unique and First Ever" the invitations had promised. It would have to be at dinner, they guessed.

How right they were.

Another black cloth stretched across the wide expanse of the dinner table criss-crossed by wide, silvery satin ribbons. Snowy napery graced each place setting and white roses, gleaming silver, crystal goblets and a colorful scattering of porcelain birds completed the decor. After the guests were seated and the wine was poured, the lights of the magnificent Venetian chandelier were dimmed and all conversation stopped as a breathless hush fell over the dining salon. The candles flickered in the slight draft that was created when the door to the kitchen swung open. Four white-tie-and-tails-clad waiters carried heavy, large silver trays stacked with — the very latest of supermarket convenience — *Swanson's TV Dinners* still in their original metal trays. White-gloved hands gently plopped a serving on each of the guests' gold and cobalt-blue Rosenthal plates. Heads held erect, with backs stiff and straight, the waiters left the stunned silence of the dining room. The swinging doors flapped shut, and one could have heard that proverbial pin drop.

Cool and collected, without a glance at her guests, Agatha picked up her knife and fork, and as though she'd been served with a fine *vol au volent,* she proceeded to eat her dinner. In stunned silence her guests followed suit.

Fortunately, one irresponsible soul unsuccessfully tried to hide her amusement, then interrupted the subdued moment by letting go with a barrage of irresistible shrieks of laughter. Soon the table rocked, Agatha's eyes flashed appreciative bolts of mirth at her guests, and between bouts of laughter she promised her friends an equally unique dessert.

You guessed it.

When the pithy remains of the main course in their tinny tin cans were cleared, the four well-dressed waiters reappeared, and placed a heavy crystal dessert plate in front of each guest with a paper-wrapped *Eskimo Pie* resting in its center.

Agatha had outdone herself.

World's Best Pork Chops

Ingredients:

6   pork chops, 1-1/2 inches thick

Marinade:
1-1/2   cups vegetable oil
3/4   cup soy sauce
1/4   cup Worcestershire sauce
1/3   cup lemon juice
1/2   cup red wine vinegar
2   tablespoons dry mustard
1-1/2   teaspoons salt
1   tablespoon pepper
2   cloves garlic, crushed
1-1/2   tablespoons fresh parsley,
          chopped

❋ Combine marinade ingredients in large jar. Shake well. Place pork chops in glass baking dish or marinade container. Pour marinade over chops; cover and refrigerate overnight. The next morning, turn chops and return to refrigerator until ready to grill. Let come to room temperature.

❋ Using direct heat, grill chops for about 7 minutes on each side.

❋ Serves 6.

Ingredients:

3	cups dry red wine
3	cups onion, chopped
2-1/4	cups soy sauce
3/4	cup olive oil
8	large cloves garlic, chopped
1	tablespoon plus 1-1/2 teaspoons dry mustard
1	tablespoon plus 1-1/2 teaspoons ground ginger
6	large bell peppers, all varieties and colors, cut into 3/4-inch-wide strips
4	large red onions, cut into 1/2-inch rings
4-1/2	pounds flank steak

Grilled French Rolls:

18	large French bread rolls
3/4	cup olive oil
7	cloves garlic, flattened pepper to taste

Grilled Flank Steak, Onion and Bell Pepper Sandwiches

❋ Combine first 7 ingredients in a large bowl. Divide steaks, bell peppers and red onions among large shallow pans. Cover with marinade, turn to coat. Cover and refrigerate for 6 to 8 hours. Prepare barbecue (high heat). Drain steaks and vegetables. Grill steaks to your taste, about 4 minutes per side for rare. Transfer to platter. Grill vegetables to light brown, about 4 minutes per side. Slice steaks thinly across grain and arrange steaks and vegetables on large platter. Serve with grilled French rolls.

❋ Grilled French Rolls:
❋ Preheat oven to broil.
❋ Heat olive oil in a heavy skillet over medium-low heat, add garlic and sauté until light brown, about 4 minutes. Discard garlic. Split rolls open in half, place on foil-lined cookie sheets, brush with garlic-flavored oil, sprinkle with pepper. Place under broiler in center of oven, oiled side down, until golden brown. Serve hot or at room temperature.
❋ Serves 12.

❋ Note: You can simmer the marinade over medium low heat for 20 minutes and serve as an "au jus" with the sandwiches.

Pride Takes a Tumble

The day of the Gourmet Food Gala Extravaganza had finally arrived. Being the chair — the head of the event — had been quite a social "plum" for Judith, and she had spent endless hours planning the charity affair. She worked hard and often got herself into a nervous tizzy which invariably brought on an annoying attack of the hiccups. She was a perfectionist to the nth degree. Everything had to be just right. After all, one event done well could mean another event done better. Who knows where that could lead?

In the process Judith had managed to drive several of her committees to tears, barely escaped a hair-pulling riot and had a few serious battles with the catering department of the luxury hotel where the event was to take place. Two owners of the participating vineyards regretted ever having committed to supply the wine for the gala, and several of the chefs involved with food displays were in an uproar. All of a sudden, Judith emerged as a self-appointed connoisseur of food and fine wines, told the florist how to arrange flowers, and asked the resident hotel manager to be sure to dress in black tie (the man had no intention of attending). Judith had managed to alienate just about everyone connected with the event.

Getting herself ready for the gala night had included everything from a massage, a manicure and a pedicure to a fancy hairdo and, of course, the extravagant velvet gown from New York. Her personal agenda consisted of one thing only — to outshine the rest of the world.

Arriving at the hotel early to survey the ballroom one last time before the several hundred guests made their entrance, she noticed that some silly decorating assistant had put up balloons in the room she had spent hours decorating to perfection earlier in the day with the help of the florist and his assistants. Judith despised balloons, and, seething, she went off in the direction of the escalator to search for Larry, the lighting guy she had hired for the event. He would have to find a ladder and a couple of pins for her; she was going to get rid of those offending balloons. By gosh and by gala, she'd do the job herself!

With her head in the clouds, and her mind on the offending balloons, she rode the escalator down to the lobby. Unfortunately, she had neglected to gather up the many yards of her black velvet skirt, which trailed in generous folds behind her. As she stepped off the escalator, an accident happened. The regal cascade of velvet got stuck in the metal jaws of the unforgiving moving staircase. The force of the running stairs eating up her gown pulled Judith down to her knees as she yanked at the disappearing fabric, yelling frantically for help.

The scene caused quite a stir in the lobby; there was little anyone could do to save her skirt or her dignity. Hearing the commotion from his post at the entry, Larry rushed to her rescue, and with his pocketknife chopped away what was left of her skirt. When Judith looked up from her ridiculous kneeling position on the lobby's marble floor, she started to hiccup violently as she came face to face with the members of her committees, with their every hair in place and their elegant gowns flowing softly to the floor.

Between body-jerking hiccups, Judith managed an embarrassed crooked grin as she got to her feet with the help of Larry. She checked the hem of her once-upon-a-time long gown, which now barely reached her knees and had that crazy, raggedy, zig-zaggy look that only Daisy Mae could appreciate. The committee members murmured some words of condolence and left her to her own doing.

With nothing else to change into, she pulled herself together, stuck out her chin and carried on as if the gown had been designed to have that shredded, wild look even Gaultier would have envied. Some say that after her pride took a tumble, Judith mended her ways — others say she just wears miniskirts to galas now. Oh, she's also taking breathing lessons to overcome hiccuping.

Gala Vegetable Strudel

Ingredients:

1   sheet prepared strudel dough, defrosted

Filling:
2   tablespoons olive oil
2   tablespoons butter
1   medium onion, finely sliced
1   clove garlic, minced
1/2   green bell pepper, cut into thin strips
1/2   red bell pepper, cut into thin strips
1/2   pound mushrooms, sliced thin
1/2   yellow zucchini, sliced thin
4   ounces sharp cheddar, shredded
1   tablespoon butter, melted
1/2   teaspoon thyme
      Salt and pepper to taste

❀ Heat half of oil and butter in heavy skillet, sauté onion and garlic until soft. Remove from skillet to paper towel. Heat rest of oil and butter, sauté peppers, mushrooms and zucchini until slightly softened, about 6 minutes. Remove from heat.

❀ Preheat oven to 350.

❀ Assembly:

❀ Roll out pastry sheet on slightly floured board, adding about one to two inches to each side. In center of sheet, arrange vegetable mixture; top with onion, then cheese. Carefully fold short ends over filling; fold opposites over filling and roll up jelly-roll fashion. Place strudel seam down on baking sheet, brush with additional butter.

❀ Bake strudel about 30 minutes until golden brown. Cool slightly.

❀ Can be prepared one day ahead, refrigerated and brought to room temperature before baking.

❀ Serves 4 to 6.

Grilled Marinated Lamb

Ingredients:

4	fresh lamb chops, trimmed of fat
4	cloves garlic, crushed
4	sprigs fresh rosemary
2	teaspoons soy sauce
1/4	cup olive oil
1	teaspoon cracked black pepper
4	thin slices fresh ginger
	Dijon mustard for dipping

❀ Combine all ingredients except mustard in a glass bowl, add lamb. Cover tightly and refrigerate. Marinate for at least 24 hours, turning meat several times.

❀ Next day, grill over hot coals or in a very hot cast iron skillet, 3 minutes on each side for medium rare. Serve with Dijon mustard.

❀ Serves 4.

Parmesan Salmon

Ingredients:

4	salmon fillets
2	sticks butter, melted
1	cup Parmesan cheese
1	teaspoon garlic powder
1/2	teaspoon dill weed

❀ Put fillets in a foil "basket" with turned up edges. Pour melted butter over fish. Sprinkle with spices and Parmesan cheese. Refrigerate 1 hour to form crust. Grill on barbeque in foil basket for 20 to 25 minutes; do not turn.

❀ Serves 4.

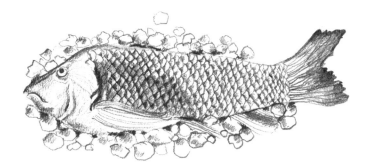

Chicken Pot Pie

Ingredients:

3	boneless skinless chicken breasts
1/2	teaspoon garlic salt
1	teaspoon black pepper
2	cans (10-1/2-ounce) cream of chicken soup, divided
1	can (15-ounce) chicken broth
1	large potato, peeled and chopped
1/2	cup celery, chopped
1	cup carrot, chopped
3/4	cup yellow onion, chopped
1/2	cup mushrooms, sliced
1/2	cup frozen peas
1/4	teaspoon cayenne pepper (optional)

Pie Crust:

3	cups flour
1	teaspoon salt
1/3	cup shortening
2/3	cup butter
1	egg
1	tablespoon vinegar
1/3	cup water

＊ Preheat oven to 350 degrees.

＊ Season chicken with garlic salt and 1/2 teaspoon black pepper, place in baking dish, cover with 1 can cream of chicken soup. Cover with foil and bake for 45 to 60 minutes. Remove from pan, cube, and return to baking dish.

＊ Boil potato, celery, carrots and onion in chicken broth until tender. Turn off heat, add mushrooms, peas and cayenne pepper. Fold in chicken mixture. Add second can of cream of chicken soup.

＊ Crust:

＊ Blend flour, salt, shortening and butter in a food processor. Add egg, vinegar and water to food processor, blend well.

＊ Preheat oven to 425 degrees.

＊ Divide dough in half; roll out on floured cutting board. Place one crust on bottom of pie pan, fill with chicken mixture, top with second crust, crimp edges. Cut a few slits in top crust and bake for 35 to 40 minutes. Let cool for 5 to 10 minutes after baking.

＊ Yields one 10-inch or 4 to 6 individual pies.

The Boston Flasher

Early-morning runs along the Charles River are a tradition for all sorts of Bostonians: the rich, the poor, the students, the professionals, the ugly, the beautiful, the clothed and the naked. The *naked*? Yes, the naked. It wasn't only the sight of youthful bodies rowing their way upriver back to Harvard that greeted Julie each morning along the Charles. It was a very handsome, trim man in his forties, a banker sort, she thought, who decided to show her his — well, you know what.

A *flasher*! The Boston Flasher, you could say. Half asleep, Julie was awakened from her time of meditation not by a jolt of coffee, but by this guy showing her his Willy! Julie actually called the police once to report the incident, but when no one got too excited about it, she quickly decided she needed to take matters into her own hands. She needed to get this pesky show-off on camera; she needed proof! Hell, she was a news producer, she knew how to document a story as it was happening. She was determined to get this flasher red-handed. (Maybe red-handed wasn't the best word in this type of situation.)

It was all set. Garvin, a fellow journalist, was going to run behind her with a camera acting the paparazzo. As Julie passed the flasher, Garvin was to come from behind and snap a photo of the nut. Julie was excited just thinking about her first sting operation. She was determined to get it right, and get the guy. She hadn't figured out just how she would present the "exposé" to the public, but was certain there'd be a way.

The two journalists set out on their way one beautiful blue and bright Boston morning. The camera was full of film and the two were abuzz with excitement. So what if it wasn't Nixon and Watergate — it was their own little Willy-By-The-Water scandal. With well-paced jogging steps, Julie approached the flasher's favorite performance area under the bridge with her heart racing. She casually looked back to make sure Garvin was behind her. By the time she got to the bridge, her heart was ready to jump out of her body and swim back up to Harvard with all the crew teams.

This was it! She turned the corner ready to face the flasher and his little friend one more time. She stopped dead in her tracks. After all these many days of encountering this offensive soul, the man wasn't there. The flasher hadn't shown up! What a blooming disappointment. All that adrenaline had gone to naught.

Julie and Garvin had planned a party for that night to "unveil" the flasher unveiling himself. But since they didn't have any scandalous photos to reveal, they celebrated the unsuccessful sting operation with some good food. In memory of the phantom flasher, Julie created a whole new chicken dish and aptly named it No-Peek Chicken.

No-Peek Baked Chicken

Ingredients:

1	box prepared long grain wild rice with herbs mix
2	cans cream of mushroom soup
1	can cream of broccoli soup
1	can plus 6 ounces cold water
1	cup long grain rice
1	teaspoon dried parsley
1	teaspoon savory
1	can water chestnuts
1	clove garlic, minced
6	boneless, skinless chicken breast halves
1	package onion soup mix, divided

❀ Preheat oven to 350 degrees.
❀ Combine all ingredients except chicken and half package of soup mix in a 9 x 13 inch baking dish. Add chicken pieces and top all with remaining dry soup mix. Bake covered for 2 hours. Don't peek!
❀ Serves 4 to 6.

Chicken Cacciatore

Ingredients:

4	boneless, skinless chicken breast halves
2	tablespoons olive oil
1	can (32-ounce) chopped Italian-style tomatoes, undrained
1	large onion, cut thinly into rings
2	chicken bouillon cubes
2	teaspoons oregano
2	teaspoons basil
	pepper to taste
3	cloves garlic, chopped
2	medium potatoes, peeled and cubed
2	zucchinis, chopped

✱ In a medium saucepan, brown chicken in oil on both sides (for about 8 to 10 minutes). Add tomatoes, onions, bouillon, spices and garlic. Bring to a boil, reduce heat and simmer covered for 45 minutes. Add potatoes and zucchinis and cook for 30 minutes or until vegetables are tender. Serve over favorite pasta, couscous, or rice.

✱ Serves 4 to 6.

Aunt Kaye's Fantastic Feta Chicken

Ingredients:

6   boneless, skinless chicken breast halves

2   tablespoons fresh-squeezed lemon juice, divided

2   teaspoons chopped fresh oregano (or 1 teaspoon dried)

1/2 teaspoon fresh black pepper

6   ounces feta cheese

* Preheat oven to 350 degrees.

* Place chicken in a 9 x 13 inch glass dish sprayed with nonfat cooking spray. Drizzle with 1 tablespoon lemon juice. Sprinkle with oregano and pepper. Top with Feta. Drizzle last 1 tablespoon of lemon juice over all. Cover with foil and bake for 45 minutes (take foil off for last 10 minutes).

* Serves 4 to 6.

* <u>Note</u>: Try serving over Orzo pasta. Follow pasta cooking instructions on package, substituting chicken broth for water.

Baked Chicken and Stuffing

Ingredients:

6	boneless, skinless chicken breast halves
1	can cream of chicken soup, undiluted
1	cup mayonnaise
1	tablespoon lemon juice
1/2	teaspoon curry powder
1/2	cup cheddar cheese, shredded
1	cup Pepperidge Farm Stuffing Mix, crushed

❀ Preheat oven to 350 degrees.
❀ Place chicken on bottom of ungreased 8 X 12 inch baking dish. In a small bowl, combine soup, mayonnaise, lemon juice, curry, and cheese; spread over chicken. Sprinkle stuffing on top. Bake for 45 minutes.
❀ Serves 4.
❀ Can be prepared a day ahead, refrigerated and brought to room temperature before baking.

Chicken With Lemon Wine Sauce

Ingredients:

6	boneless, skinless chicken breast halves
1	cup flour
1	teaspoon salt
1	teaspoon pepper
1/2	stick butter
2/3	cup dry white wine
1/4	cup lemon juice
3	tablespoons capers

❀ Pound chicken breasts to 1/4-inch thickness. Mix flour, salt and pepper in Ziploc bag; add chicken and shake to coat. In heavy skillet melt butter, cook coated chicken for 2 to 3 minutes on each side, covered, over medium heat. Add wine and lemon juice. Cook until slightly thickened and cooked through, about 15 to 20 minutes. Top with capers.

Grilled Marinated Chicken

Ingredients:

6	boneless, skinless chicken breast halves
1/3	cup olive oil
3	cloves garlic, chopped
1/2	teaspoon salt
1/2	cup brown sugar
3	tablespoons grainy mustard
1/2	cup cider vinegar
	Juice of 1 lime
	Juice of 1/2 lemon
1/4	teaspoon pepper

❀ Combine marinade ingredients. Place chicken in glass baking dish and coat well with marinade. Cover.

❀ Marinate chicken breasts overnight. Remove from refrigerator 1 hour before barbequing. Grill approximately 8 minutes on each side or until cooked through. This marinade is excellent for pork, steaks, ribs, and other cuts of meat.

Paella

Ingredients:

2	sticks butter, divided
6	cloves garlic, minced and divided
2	pounds skinless, boneless chicken breast, cut into chunks
3	cups regular white rice
1/2	teaspoon saffron
1/2	large yellow onion, chopped
1	red pepper, seeded and chopped
6 – 7	cups canned chicken broth
1/4	teaspoon salt
1/2	teaspoon pepper
3	small Chorizo sausages
3/4	cup pimentos, diced
2	dozen large shrimp, rinsed, peeled, tails still attached
1-1/2	dozen clams
1-1/2	dozen mussels
	Lobster lovers may add 2 lobster tails

✿ Preheat oven to 350 degrees.

✿ In a large saucepan, melt 1 stick butter, add 2 cloves minced garlic. Heat until foaming, sauté chicken chunks. When chicken is golden brown (about 20 minutes), remove from pan and set aside. In the remaining juices, sauté 3 cloves minced garlic, 1/2 stick butter and rice on medium heat for about 5 minutes. Add saffron, onions and red pepper. Sauté and stir for 5 to 8 minutes. Add chicken broth, bring to a boil. Season with salt and pepper. Reduce heat to low, and cook rice uncovered for 20 minutes.

✿ In a separate pan, cook the sausages until slightly firm. Remove sausages with a slotted spoon and slice diagonally into 1-inch pieces. Mix sausages with chicken pieces and add pimentos. Add these to cooked rice mixture in large saucepan. This portion can be prepared well in advance.

✿ Sauté shrimp in a saucepan on medium heat with 1 clove minced garlic and 1/2 stick butter for 5 to 7 minutes. Set aside.

✿ Place rice mixture in uncovered paella pan. Bake in oven for approximately 20 to 25 minutes. Add more chicken broth if needed. Add shrimp, clams, mussels (and lobster tails if used) and cook until clams open and shellfish is pink, about 4 more minutes. Don't overcook the paella, or it will dry out quickly. If this happens, add more chicken broth.

✿ Serves 6 to 8.

Chinese Noodles – Seto Style

Ingredients:

1	box Rose brand noodles (Asian food section)
1/2	cup vegetable oil
1	pound chicken, cubed
1	cup oyster sauce, divided
1/2	cup light Kikkoman soy sauce
1/2	cup sesame oil, divided

Toppings:

1	large bunch broccoli, cut into large bite-size pieces
1	bunch green onions, chopped
1	cup fresh pea pods

❀ Heat vegetable oil in wok or large skillet; add chicken, 1/2 cup oyster sauce, soy sauce and 1/4 cup sesame oil. Cook for 15 minutes, stirring constantly. Add broccoli, sauté for 4 minutes; toss in green onions. Stir for a few more minutes. Add pea pods. Stir for 2 minutes. Remove from heat.

❀ While cooking meat and vegetables, boil a large pot of water and cook noodles according to directions; drain. Mix noodles with 1/4 cup sesame oil, add 1/2 cup oyster sauce and mix together. Toss noodles gently with chicken and vegetables and serve.

❀ Serves 4.

Wheeler-Dealer Shrimp

When Martha was teaching at a junior high school in a small town in Louisiana, she met some interesting characters and one rather questionable one — all of them rather entertaining. The one who deeply puzzled her, but who she found downright amusing, was one of the athletic coaches, who she swore had big-time Mafia connections. Why? Well, why would a coach spend more than half his time on the telephone? He also had some suspicious-looking friends who came around at odd hours, wearing dark suits and matching "shades" and carrying leather brief-cases. Always giving people names she believed to be more fitting their demeanor, she had affixed to the young man the code name "Valentino."

Incurably curious, with a rather highly developed CIA character trait, Martha let her suspicions become her guide. Short of stalking the man, she investigated his movements, and tried her darnedest to find out if Valentino was indeed involved in shady dealings. She was not at all surprised when she discovered that he was using the telephone for bookmaking, and his friends appeared to be bagmen for the "man." Criminal activity in the pristine setting of a rural junior high school? What indeed was the world coming to?

No sooner had she decided to turn her "case" over to the D.A., than "Valentino" disappeared from the scene. Four of his dark-suited friends had shown up at the school early one morning, and with overly friendly gestures had muscled him into the interior of a long, black and sinister-looking limousine. He never returned to school. Coaching may have interfered with his real work. Martha had witnessed the event to which she referred as "the abduction of Valentino."

However, before he split the scene, he had given Martha a recipe for a shrimp dish which he swore came from a famous chef of a famous restaurant frequented by (in)famous people. Martha never had a doubt that she had acquired a high-class-low-life stolen recipe that was excellent. It would have to be. People like Valentino and his friends in their dark suits and matching limousines expected the best — or else!

Marinated Shrimp Valentino

Ingredients:

50 – 60	medium raw shrimp, rinsed well, beheaded, shells on
1	stick butter
1/3	cup Worcestershire Sauce
1/2	teaspoon salt
1	teaspoon black pepper
1	teaspoon thyme
1/2	teaspoon celery salt
1	teaspoon cayenne pepper (half if less spicy dish desired)
2	teaspoons rosemary
2	teaspoons garlic puree (prepared)
1	tablespoon olive oil

❀ Melt butter in large skillet, add all other ingredients except shrimp. Mix well, simmer (do not boil) for 8 to 10 minutes. Remove from heat. Let sauce cool before adding shrimp. Transfer shrimp with sauce to 4-quart baking dish. Refrigerate for 3 hours or overnight.

❀ Preheat oven to 400 degrees.

❀ To serve, let come to room temperature, bake for 18 to 20 minutes at 400 degrees.

❀ Serves 4 to 6.

Sausage and Porcini Mushroom Polenta

Ingredients:

Sauce:

2	tablespoons olive oil
2	cups porcini mushrooms
1	medium yellow onion, chopped
1/2	pound ground pork sausage
1/2	pound ground mild Italian sausage
4	cloves garlic, minced
1/3	cup red wine
1/3	cup cooking sherry
2	cups chicken broth
2	cups tomato sauce
2	teaspoons dry parsley
2	teaspoons dry basil
1	teaspoon thyme
1	teaspoon salt
1/2	teaspoon white pepper
1/2	teaspoon black pepper
1/2	teaspoon red pepper flakes
12	ounces tomato paste
1	red pepper, chopped
1	yellow pepper, chopped
1	pound Italian link sausages

Garnish:

1-1/4	cups Parmesan, freshly shredded

Polenta:

2	cups polenta (cornmeal)
6	cups boiling water
1	teaspoon salt
1	cups Parmesan cheese

❋ Sauce:

❋ In large heavy skillet, sauté mushrooms (if dried, follow directions on package first) in olive oil for 5 to 7 minutes. Remove mushrooms to small bowl, set aside. In leftover oil in skillet, brown onion with both ground sausages. Add garlic, drain fat and add wine. Add sherry. Stir well. Add chicken broth, tomato sauce, all spices, tomato paste, peppers, and sautéed mushrooms, simmer 1 hour.

❋ While sauce is simmering, brown link sausage in small saucepan until cooked through. Set aside.

❋ Polenta:

❋ In a large saucepan, slowly add polenta to boiling water and add salt. Reduce to medium heat. Stir for 5 minutes. Add 1 cup Parmesan cheese while stirring. Place in a large casserole dish coated with nonstick cooking spray, top with sauce. Bake for 30 Add link sausage atop sauce for the last 10 minutes

❋ Sprinkle shredded Parmesan cheese on top and serve.

❋ Serves 6 to 8.

Delectable Desserts

Motto for living life:
"Eat dessert before dinner; why waste the calories on salad?"

J. K. Morse

The Forgotten Ingredient

Dorothy would never have left Kansas had she ever had a taste of Eileen Warden's "Crepes Divine." By the same token, none of Eileen's friends ever left the state without the recipe for her luscious designer pancakes safely tucked away in her luggage along with the family treasures. The recipe was by no means a casual handout by its originator. Wily, crafty Eileen only handed over the instructions for the preparation of Crepes Divine when one of her friends was transferred and moved away — preferably abroad, perhaps even China or Timbuktu.

In the fading moments of the very last so-long-goodbye-*au-revoir* dinner party for the departing best friend, Eileen would reluctantly hand over a gaily decorated envelope closed tightly against invaders with superglue. The envelope was inscribed with a threat in her bold handwriting: "Recipe will self-destruct if envelope is opened before your first dinner party in your new home."

Orders for transfers from the powerful conglomerate Eileen's husband and friends worked for, were rescinded every once in a while, and the person stayed in place — forever. To guard herself against such an event, Eileen would "accidentally" forget to include a major ingredient from the recipe and, on top of that, give at least one incorrect measure for another. She wasn't about to have perfect Crepes Divine appear on someone else's dinner table right there in Kansas City. Oh, no! She took out insurance.

Only after the transferee had settled into her new home, and was sure not to return to Kansas, did one of those clever, gay little notes from Eileen arrive, apologizing for the computer having made a mistake with the recipe and herewith offering the corrected version of Crepes Divine. I believe it's about time this recipe came out of Kansas and out of the closet.

Shucks, Eileen, you're just not in Kansas anymore!

Eileen's Crepes Divine

Ingredients:

Crepes:

3	whole eggs
1-1/2	cups flour
1/2	cup regular milk
2	tablespoons Courvoissier or fine brandy
1	teaspoon sugar
1	tablespoon melted butter
1/2	teaspoon salt
2 – 4	tablespoons melted butter for cooking crepes

Filling:

1	can (16-ounce) dark cherries, pitted, well-drained* (reserve juice)
3/4	cup sour cream
4	tablespoons sugar
1	tablespoon Courvoissier
1	teaspoon vanilla

Sauce:

	reserved cherry juice
2	tablespoons lemon juice
2	tablespoons crystallized ginger, finely chopped
1-1/2	tablespoons cornstarch
1	tablespoon Courvoissier

❀ Put eggs, flour, milk, sugar and salt into a mixing bowl, beat and blend with a wire whisk until smooth; mix in Courvoissier. Add melted butter, blend well.

❀ Use pastry brush to lightly apply melted butter to heavy 8-inch skillet before making each crepe. Heat butter but do not burn; add approximately 4 tablespoons batter with a small ladle, swirl pan to evenly distribute the batter by filling out the pan. Cook over medium heat for about 30 seconds, with spatula flip crepe onto other side; cook for about 12 seconds. Turn crepe out onto a platter; cover with wax paper piece to separate from next crepe. Continue making crepes until batter is gone.

❀ Makes about 14 crepes. Recipe can be doubled easily.

❀ In a medium bowl beat sour cream with sugar and vanilla; add Courvoissier and well-drained cherries.

❀ Place three tablespoons of filling in center of each crepe, roll, place face down on platter.

❀ Dissolve cornstarch in lemon juice. In a small saucepan, bring reserved cherry juice to soft boil; add cornstarch mixture, reduce heat to low, stir well to avoid clumping. Remove from heat, add ginger and Courvoissier. Drizzle a generous table-spoon of sauce over each individual serving of crepes.

❀ All three parts of this delicious dessert can be made a day ahead, kept refrigerated and brought to room temperature before serving. Reheat sauce in microwave and drizzle over crepes.

*Note: Drain cherries in sieve overnight. If cherries are not well-drained, the sour cream filling will turn runny, discolored, and hard to handle.

Tiramisu

Ingredients:

5	eggs, divided
5	tablespoons sugar
500	grams (about 1 pound, 2 ounces) mascarpone cheese
16–20	ounces liquid espresso coffee
2	tablespoons Cognac
2	teaspoons sugar
2	packages champagne Italian lady fingers
1	cup chocolate shavings (semi-sweet or bittersweet)

❀ Separate eggs. Beat yolks with sugar very well, then add mascarpone and beat again.

❀ Beat egg whites until stiff. Gently fold whites into above mixture.

❀ Make espresso (you may use instant espresso, or three regular cups of strong coffee will do.) Add cognac and sugar.

❀ Dip one package ladyfingers into coffee mixture until lightly soaked and place in bottom of 10 x 10 inch glass dish. Spread half of mascarpone mixture on top and then sprinkle with 1/2 cup chocolate shavings. Dip remaining ladyfingers. Repeat layers. Chill well before serving. Individual dishes work well too.

❀ Serves 6 to 8.

Burnt Crème

Ingredients:

1	pint whipping cream
4	egg yolks
1/2	cup granulated sugar
1	tablespoon vanilla
1	tablespoon sugar, divided

❀ Preheat oven to 350 degrees.

❀ Heat cream over low heat until bubbles form around edge, about 10 minutes. Beat egg yolks and sugar together until mixture is pale yellow; gradually beat in cream. Stir in vanilla and pour into 6 individual 6-ounce custard cups (three quarters of the way full). Place custard cups in baking pan that has 1/2 inch water in bottom. Bake until set, approximately 45 minutes. Remove custard cups and refrigerate until chilled. After chilled sprinkle each custard with 1/2 teaspoon sugar. Place on top rack of oven, broil until topping is medium brown. Watch very closely! This will take a minute or less. Chill before serving.

❀ Serves 6.

Pear Pie

Ingredients:

4 – 6	pears, peeled and quartered
2/3	cup sugar
1/2	stick butter
1/4	cup flour
1	teaspoon vanilla
2	eggs, beaten
1	single pie crust (homemade or premade)

❀ Preheat oven to 400 degrees.
❀ In a pie pan arrange pie dough, add pears. Mix rest of ingredients, pour over pears. Bake at 400 degrees for 15 minutes; reduce heat to 350 degrees and bake pie for 45 minutes more.
❀ Serves 6 to 8.

Fabulous Frosting with Angel Food Cake

Ingredients:

1-1/2	cups sugar
6	tablespoons Droste (if possible) cocoa
1	pint whipping cream
1	teaspoon vanilla
1	pinch salt
1	angel food cake

❀ Mix together sugar, cocoa and whipping cream in large mixing bowl, cover, keep refrigerated overnight.

❀ Next day bake angel food cake or purchase cake at grocer. Cool cake thoroughly before frosting.

❀ Chill beaters in freezer for a few minutes. Remove frosting mixture from refrigerator. Before beating, add vanilla and salt to mixture. Beat until frosting is thick.

❀ Frost cake and refrigerate until ready to serve.

❀ Serves 8.

Banana Bread

Ingredients:

1/4	cup vegetable oil
1/3	cup packed brown sugar
1/3	cup granulated sugar
2	eggs, beaten
4	ripe bananas, mashed
1	cup chopped nuts (walnuts or almonds work well)
1	cup dried fruit (cranberries, blueberries, apricots or currants)
2	cups flour
1	teaspoon baking soda
1/2	teaspoon salt

- ❊ Preheat oven to 350 degrees.
- ❊ Beat oil with brown sugar and white sugar until creamy; add eggs, bananas. Add fruit and nuts. Sift flour with salt and baking soda; add to mixture. Stir well. Grease and flour two small loaf pans and pour in mixture. Bake for 1 hour.

Zucchini Bread

✸ Preheat oven to 350 degrees.
✸ Combine all ingredients in a bowl and stir until well blended. Grease and flour 4 small loaf pans or 2 large ones, and pour in mixture. Bake for 1 hour or until done.

Ingredients:

3	cups regular flour
3	eggs
2-1/4	cups sugar
1	cup oil
2	cups zucchini, grated
1	tablespoon vanilla
1	teaspoon baking soda
1	teaspoon salt
1	teaspoon cinnamon
1/2	teaspoon baking powder
1	tablespoon orange rind
4	peach halves, cut into pieces
1	cup nuts (optional)

Ingredients:

1	cup sugar
2	whole eggs
1	cup sour cream
1-1/3	cups regular flour, unsifted
1/2	teaspoon salt
1/3	cup powdered cocoa
1	teaspoon baking soda
1	tablespoon butter, melted
1/2	teaspoon vanilla

Frosting:

1/4	cup powdered cocoa
2	cups powdered sugar
1/4	cup cream
1/2	teaspoon salt
1	tablespoon plus 1 teaspoon liquid coffee or espresso (prepared beverage)
1/2	cup walnuts, chopped (optional)

Fern Morse's Quick Chocolate Cake

❀ Preheat oven to 350 degrees.

❀ By hand, beat eggs and sugar until mixture turns pale yellow; add sour cream. In a separate bowl sift flour, salt, cocoa and baking soda chocolate together; add to egg mixture. Fold in melted butter and vanilla; stir until well mixed. Turn into a greased flat square or rectangular pan and bake until just done. Do not over bake. Allow 25 minutes in a 10 X 10 inch square pan or a 7-1/2 X 12 inch glass pan. Test with toothpick. When toothpick comes out clean, cake is done. Cool.

❀ Frosting:

❀ By hand, mix cocoa, powdered sugar, cream, salt and coffee, until the right consistency to spread is reached. You may need to add a little extra cream to thin or powdered sugar to thicken frosting. Top with walnuts.

❀ Serves 12 to 15, depending on size of pieces.

Oregon Trail Raw Apple Cake

Ingredients:

4	cups apples, unpeeled, chopped
2	eggs
2	cups sugar
2	teaspoons cinnamon
1/2	cup vegetable oil
1	cup nuts, chopped
2	cups flour
2	teaspoons baking soda
1/2	teaspoon salt
1/4	cup powdered sugar

❀ Preheat oven to 350 degrees.

❀ In a large mixing bowl, blend all ingredients except apples and powdered sugar with a hand mixer on medium speed. Stir in apples by hand. Pour into a greased and floured bundt pan and bake for 50 to 55 minutes. Let cool for 10 minutes. Turn cake onto a cake plate; sprinkle with powdered sugar.

"*...Life's Short, Eat Dessert First...*"

Those are fighting words, and could easily have originated from my husband Jim's approach to eating. Jim insists the most effective way to lose weight is to eat dessert before dinner. "Why waste all those calories on a salad," he says with tongue in cheek. Lucky Jim! He stands six feet, three inches tall, weighs a trim 170 pounds, and comes from a family that lays claim to possessing a roadrunner-high-speed metabolism. They have the slogan "A little dessert never hurt anyone" silk-screened on their running shorts.

I had quite an introduction to that kind of dieting when I spent my first weekend with Jim's family in Central Oregon. It was a memorable experience. Early in the morning, the men walked to the little country store for the Sunday paper, which was doled out to various members of the family in sections. As we were sitting in the sun-filled living room reading and trading sections, every once in a while someone would quietly leave the peaceful family circle and reappear with a huge piece of chocolate cake in one hand. What? No breakfast?

I headed for the kitchen, where I discovered a cookie sheet in the middle of the kitchen counter on which rested the remains of what must have been a huge chocolate cake. Just then one of my in-laws appeared, disregarding my presence, swooped up a piece of cake without breaking his stride, kept reading his paper and headed back to the living room, making room for the next customer. She, too, swooped up a hunk of cake, which left just one more piece of "Swooping Cake."

To heck with grapefruit and cereal, never mind the wheat toast, the low-fat spread and shivering yogurt. I approached the hub of concentrated calories, and with a sure hand — just like the rest of the family — I swooped up the last sinful piece of chocolate cake. After all, a little dessert never hurt anyone.

Chocolate Swooping Cake

Ingredients:

2	cups all-purpose flour, sifted
2	cups sugar
1	teaspoon baking soda
2	teaspoons cinnamon
2	sticks margarine
1/4	cup powdered cocoa
1	cup water
1/2	cup buttermilk
2	eggs, beaten
1	teaspoon vanilla

Frosting:

1	stick margarine
1/4	cup powdered cocoa
6	tablespoons milk
2	cups powdered sugar
1	teaspoon vanilla
1/2	cup walnuts, chopped

❀ Preheat oven to 400 degrees.

❀ Combine flour, sugar, soda and cinnamon in a large mixing bowl. Combine margarine, cocoa and water and bring to a boil, remove from heat. Add hot cocoa mixture to flour mixture. Blend in buttermilk, eggs and vanilla. Mix well and pour into lightly greased jelly roll pan. Bake for 20 minutes or until toothpick comes out clean.

❀ Frosting:

❀ In a heavy pan bring to boil margarine, cocoa and milk. Remove from heat. Add powdered sugar and vanilla. Mix well and spread while cake is still warm. Sprinkle with chopped nuts.

Ingredients:

4	ounces unsweetened Baker's chocolate
2/3	cup butter
4	eggs
1/2	cup Kahlua or Kamora
1-3/4	cups granulated sugar
1	teaspoon vanilla
1-1/4	cups all-purpose flour
1	teaspoon baking powder
1	teaspoon salt
6	ounces semi-sweet chocolate chips

Frosting:
2	tablespoons Kahlua or Kamora
1	teaspoon instant coffee
1	stick butter, softened
2	cups powdered sugar
1/2	teaspoon vanilla extract
1	tablespoon milk

Topping:
1	ounce semi-sweet chocolate
1	tablespoon butter

Extras:
	vanilla ice cream
1	cup raspberries
1/2	cup Hershey's chocolate syrup

Nancy's Rainy Day Brownie Dessert

❀ Brownies:

❀ Preheat oven to 350 degrees.

❀ In a medium saucepan over low heat, melt unsweetened chocolate with butter. Remove pan from heat and mix in eggs, Kahlua, sugar and vanilla. Stir in flour, baking powder and salt; add chocolate chips. Spread in a greased and lightly floured 9 x 13 inch pan. Bake for 25 to 30 minutes or until edges begin to pull away from sides of pan. Cool at least 30 minutes before the next step.

❀ Frosting:

❀ In a small bowl, mix Kahlua with instant coffee, stirring until coffee is dissolved. In a medium bowl, cream butter, powdered sugar and vanilla together. Add coffee mixture and beat until well blended. Add milk to desired consistency. Spread frosting evenly over cooled brownies. For best results, refrigerate for 30 minutes before finishing with topping.

❀ Topping:

❀ In a small saucepan, melt chocolate and butter together. Cool slightly, then drizzle topping over frosting. Cool until chocolate is set. For easy cutting, refrigerate 30 minutes.

❀ Serve in a bowl with ice cream and a few raspberries and drizzle with chocolate syrup.

Caramel Layered Chocolate Squares

Ingredients:

1	package (14-ounce) light caramels
1/2	cup evaporated milk
1	package German chocolate cake mix
1-1/2	sticks butter, melted
1/3	cup evaporated milk
1	cup walnuts, chopped
1	cup semi-sweet chocolate pieces

❋ Preheat oven to 350 degrees.

❋ In a heavy saucepan, combine caramels and 1/2 cup evaporated milk. Over low heat, stir constantly until melted, set aside. Grease and flour 13 x 9 inch pan. In a large bowl combine cake mix, butter, 1/3 cup evaporated milk and walnuts. By hand, stir until dough holds together. Press 1/2 dough into pan. Bake for 6 minutes.

❋ Sprinkle 1 cup semi-sweet chocolate pieces over baked crust. Spread caramel mix over chocolate pieces. Drop rest of dough over caramel mixture. Bake an additional 15 to 18 minutes. Cool slightly, refrigerate 30 minutes, cut into 36 bars.

Marooned in Goo

What this episode taught Mary is the fact that persistence indeed pays off in all matters, even when it comes to baking cookies. A delicious macaroon recipe had been passed on to Mary from her friend Stasia. The first time Mary attempted to make the macaroons, she ended up with an extremely sticky, gooey mess that was way too sweet and stuck to her teeth. She called her batch of cookies goo balls.

She tried the recipe a second time with the same results. There was no resemblance to the delectable macaroons Stasia produced from the very same recipe. Mary finally conferred with the originator of the macaroon recipe, and neither one could figure out the problem. Mary gave it another try, and again was unsuccessful. What was consistently going wrong with the delicious morsels her friend produced with such ease?

One day, the two friends were chatting on the phone, when Stasia laughingly mentioned that she almost forgot to put the flour in the macaroon dough. Mary gasped and managed to stammer, "Flour … what flour?" She checked her friend's recipe and realized that "flour" had been accidentally omitted.

Oh, the magic of flour!

Chocolate Macaroon Cookies

Ingredients:

4	egg whites
2-1/2	cups shredded, sweetened coconut
1-1/4	cups sugar
1-1/2	tablespoons vanilla
1/2	teaspoon salt
1/4	cup plus 2 tablespoons sifted flour
1	cup bittersweet chocolate pieces

❀ Preheat oven to 300 degrees.

❀ Mix first five ingredients together in a saucepan. Heat mixture on medium temperature until smooth. Then turn up heat to medium high for three more minutes; stir constantly until mixture pulls away from pan. Remove from heat. Blend in flour.

❀ Chill mixture in a bowl covered with plastic wrap until it is cold, about 2 hours. Using a cookie dough scoop or small ice cream scoop, drop onto buttered cookie sheet. Bake for 30 to 35 minutes or until pale golden color. Wait five minutes before transferring cookies onto a cooling rack.

❀ When cookies are cool, melt chocolate over double boiler. Dip half of each cookie into melted bittersweet chocolate. Place on a cookie sheet lined with waxed paper. To expedite drying of chocolate, place cookies in the refrigerator.

❀ Makes 13 cookies.

The Third Time's the Charm

It took two decades, three meetings and some magic to make Dale and Peggy entertain serious thoughts about each other. The couple first met as teenagers when Dale, tanned to a deep bronze, was Number One lifeguard at the Greenwood Country Club, and Peggy, a Marlo Thomas look-alike, ran the snack shop. After a brief summer romance, the two young people said goodbye to each other and went off in different directions, chasing their dreams.

A decade later Dale and Peggy, both married at the time, met again at a mutual friend's lively "Tribute to Disco" party, complete with sparkling mirrors, flashing lights and all. The two boogied a little, chatted a bit, and went on their merry way. Another decade passed.

Ten years later the two old friends, then single again, met by chance over a sauté pan at a cooking class they had joined. The chef had structured the class for couples-cooking, and randomly paired Dale and Peggy off as cooking partners, unaware the two knew each other. The third time was truly the charm. They hit it off and began dating.

One day, Dale offered Peggy the use of his prize possession, a sleek, limited edition Porsche equipped with all the bells and whistles, for running her errands. No one but Dale had ever driven this little gem before, for obvious reasons. Peggy took off at sunrise, returned at sunset after having put a few miles on the odometer, and parked "Precious" on Dale's sloping driveway. She opened the trunk to retrieve her purchases, slammed the trunk shut, and walked toward the house. The jolt from the harsh slam caused the small car to lurch forward. Dale's beloved collector's edition was gathering speed at an uncontrollable rate and heading towards the open garage. It rolled in and crashed into the back wall, where it came to rest with a whining and screeching of bent metal in a shower of glass and splintered drywall.

The sports car's rear end sat in the garage; the front half, having smashed halfway through the rear wall, had landed in the wine room and knocked over a case of Cabernet Sauvignon.

Dale, who had been preparing dinner in his gourmet kitchen, came running out of the house, took one look at what had happened, rescued the unbroken bottles of wine, gave the trunk of his car a loving pat, and consoled Peggy, who was running over with apologies. He told her not to worry, everything was fixable.

What a gem, thought Peggy, as she sat across the table from him at dinner, sipping a glass of champagne, feeding on pâté de fois gras, escargots in puff pastry, lobster tails in a frothy dill and lemon sauce, and for the show stopper, a cranberry pudding.

The meal was so delicious that Peggy asked her host for the recipes. She was astounded that he declined. Maybe he was mad after all. But Dale smiled, and explained the recipes would remain a secret. As a matter of fact, he insisted they were a family secret, and unless she'd consent to become part of his family by marrying him, she'd have to go without them. This time Dale and Peggy didn't go their separate ways. That was sixteen years ago, and they lived happily ever after — together.

Some women will do anything to get their hands on a recipe.

Cranberry Bread Pudding

Ingredients:

1-1/2	cups flour, divided
1	teaspoon salt
1	teaspoon baking soda
1/2	cup molasses
1/2	cup hot water
2	cups raw cranberries (fresh or frozen)

Sauce:

1	stick butter
1/2	cup brown sugar
1/2	cup cream
1	teaspoon vanilla

❋ Into a medium bowl, sift together 1 cup flour, salt and baking soda. Add molasses and hot water. Mix in cranberries and remaining 1/2 cup flour; stir by hand. Pour into greased top of a double boiler and steam, covered, for two and a half to three hours on medium heat. Add water when double boiler runs out. To test for doneness, insert a toothpick into the center. When the toothpick comes out clean, it is done. Cool and invert onto a cake plate. Slice just before serving into 2-inch-thick individual portions.

❋ Sauce:
❋ Combine butter, brown sugar and cream in a medium pan and heat slowly until mixture bubbles. Remove from heat, stir in vanilla. Pour the hot sauce over the cranberry pudding and serve immediately.

❋ Serving suggestions:
❋ Since this tends to be an "ugly duckling" recipe, there are several ways to make it glamorous. Use a well-greased decorative mold and steam it, covered with foil, over a pot of boiling water. You can cut small sprigs of holly or evergreens and place them around the pudding on a cake plate. Before serving place one sprig of holly on each dessert plate.
❋ Serves 8.

❋ Both pudding and sauce freeze and reheat well.

Butterballs

Ingredients:

1	stick butter
1/4	cup sugar
1	cup flour
1	cup pecan pieces
1	pinch salt
1	teaspoon vanilla
2	cups powdered sugar, sifted

❀ Preheat oven to 350 degrees.

❀ Cream butter and sugar well; add flour and blend. Add salt, vanilla and pecan pieces. Mix well.

❀ Form dough into very tiny balls. Place in rows on greased cookie sheet. Bake for 7 to 8 minutes (check bottoms of cookies to avoid overbrowning). Roll butterballs in bowl of sifted powdered sugar while hot. Place on wax paper to cool. Store in airtight tins.

❀ Makes 5 to 6 dozen bite-size cookies.

Ingredients:

2	sticks butter
2	cups sugar
1	pint white Karo syrup
1	can (14-ounce) sweetened condensed milk
2-1/2	cups walnuts, chopped
2	teaspoons vanilla

Caramels

❋ Combine first 3 ingredients in a large saucepan and melt, add condensed milk, mix well. Bring to a boil on medium-high heat. Scrape bottom of pan with wooden spoon while caramels are cooking, and reduce heat to simmer until candy reaches "hard ball" stage, about 45 minutes. After caramels have been simmering for 30 minutes, test mixture every few minutes to watch for the hard ball stage.

❋ To test, fill a mug with cold water. Take a small spoonful of caramel while it is still simmering and drop into mug of water. Let it cool down for a moment, then try to form a ball with the gooey candy. The caramel is not done until the gooey ball turns into a hard ball. If you start testing at the 30-minute mark, your candy should be done after another 15 minutes or so. Be patient and your caramel will turn out perfectly.

❋ When caramel has reached hard ball stage remove pan from heat. Add walnuts and vanilla to saucepan and mix thoroughly. Turn into greased 9 x 13 inch pan and let cool. When candy is no longer warm, with kitchen scissors, cut into desired size pieces. Wrap in plastic or wax paper.

❋ Yields 80 or more inch-square pieces.

Almond Roca

Ingredients:

2	sticks butter
1	cup plus 1 tablespoon sugar
1/2	cup sliced almonds
2/3	cup semi-sweet chocolate chips, divided
1/2	cup almond dust (grind almonds in blender to make dust), divided

❀ Melt butter in heavy saucepan on medium heat until it bubbles; add sugar and let boil for 5 minutes. Stir with a wooden spoon.

❀ Add sliced almonds and boil on medium heat for 5 minutes. Pour into 9 inch Pyrex pie plate, let cool. When candy is no longer warm to touch, remove it carefully from pie plate and put on wax paper. Wipe off excess butter on both sides with paper towel.

❀ To frost almond roca, melt half chocolate chips (1/3 cup) on low heat in a small saucepan until chocolate is shiny. Spread melted chocolate onto one side of almond roca and sprinkle with half of almond dust. Let frosting dry, then turn over to other side to frost and dust. When both sides are dry, break into bite-size pieces.

❀ Makes approximately 45 to 50 large bite-size pieces.

Bare Cheesecake

Neither Laila nor Peter planned to leave the city to spend Thanksgiving with their families; they opted to spend the holiday in each other's company. Laila decided to surprise her boyfriend with a romantic Thanksgiving dinner for just the two of them. This may sound like no big deal to some women, but Laila had two obstacles blocking her way.

One, she wasn't much of a cook to begin with, and secondly, she was a staunch vegetarian committed to preparing a hearty meal for her carnivorous mate. She needed a foolproof recipe that even she couldn't goof up. Her girlfriend Meg came to the rescue and gave Laila fail-proof instructions for cooking the Thanksgiving feast. Under her friend's guidance, Laila would roast two Cornish game hens, make rosemary mashed potatoes and prepare a special mixed-greens salad using a good friend's recipe.

Laila took her time with her chores, followed directions carefully and surprised herself as she surveyed the way the meal was coming along. She also decided that she would spice up the evening a bit by meeting her boyfriend wearing only an apron and a smile. She topped herself by making Meg's famous Lite Pumpkin Cheesecake, which was the *pièce de résistance* of Laila's perfect meal. She was pleased.

To set a festive mood, she lit candles all over the house, and arranged flowers for the table, then began putting the finishing touches on the cheesecake. She had stepped back to admire her handiwork when she heard the sound of the front door falling shut. Peter was early for probably the first time in his life, but she was prepared to greet him.

She straightened her little apron, and put on her best mischievous and playful smile. As Peter was about to round the bend into the kitchen, Laila realized that something was wrong. Peter was talking to someone! Laila had almost nothing on and there was a stranger in the house. She quickly grabbed the nearest thing, which happened to be the cheesecake, and raised it chest-high to cover her bare torso just as Peter and his companion turned the corner.

She could feel herself turning bright red while praying for the proverbial floor to open and swallow her. Not only was the grinning stranger Peter's boss, but the boyfriend made matters worse by laughing out loud and saying, "That's a beautiful cheesecake you have there, darling."

She chose flight instead of fight, turned an overly exposed rear end on her guests, mumbled some sort of apology and escaped to her bedroom. After she was properly dressed and had composed herself, she rejoined the two men, hoping Peter would have the good sense to talk about the weather, or even politics.

Peter explained to her that his boss wasn't going to be able to make it home for Thanksgiving and that he, Peter, had invited him to come along for dinner on the spur of the moment. He apologized for not telling her. Laila still wished herself somewhere else on the globe, but loosened up after a couple of glasses of wine. Dinner went well, and by the time dessert came around, the men decided that their hostess had given the word "cheese"cake a new meaning.

Ingredients:

Crust:
1-1/2	cups graham cracker crumbs
3	tablespoons sugar
1/4	cup apple juice

Filling:
2	packages (8-ounce) low fat cream cheese, at room temperature
1/2	cup sugar
1/2	cup light brown sugar
4	eggs
1/3	cup nonfat milk
1-1/4	cups canned pumpkin
1/2	teaspoon cinnamon
1/8	teaspoon nutmeg
1/8	teaspoon ground cloves

Topping:
1/3	cup brown sugar
1/2	cup walnuts, chopped
1	tablespoon apple juice

Garnish:
prepared low fat Cool Whip

Bare Pumpkin Cheesecake

* Crust:
* Combine ingredients. Press cracker mixture into a greased 9-inch spring form pan and refrigerate.

* Filling:
* Preheat oven to 325 degrees.
* In a large bowl blend cream cheese and sugars together with electric mixer at high speed. Add eggs one at a time and mix thoroughly after each addition. Add remaining ingredients and mix well for 3 minutes. Pour filling into spring form pan.
* Fill jelly roll pan with 1/2 inch water, place on bottom rack of oven. Bake cheesecake on center rack for 1-1/2 hours or until knife inserted comes out clean. Turn off oven. Immediately add topping and place back in oven.

* Topping:
* Combine all ingredients in a small bowl. Sprinkle topping on baked cheesecake and return cake to cooling oven for 1/2 hour. Remove from oven, refrigerate.
* Serve well chilled with a dollop of whipped topping.

Nonna Ponzi's Biscotti

Ingredients:

2	cups sugar
2	sticks butter, melted
4	tablespoons anise seed
4	tablespoons anise flavored liqueur
3	tablespoons bourbon (or 2 teaspoons vanilla and 2 teaspoons water)
2	cups walnuts, hazelnuts or almonds, chopped
6	eggs
1	tablespoon baking powder
5-1/2	cups unbleached white flour

❀ Mix sugar with butter, anise seed, anise liqueur, bourbon and nuts. Beat in eggs. In a separate bowl, sift and measure flour, sift again with baking powder and mix into egg mixture. Blend thoroughly with sugar mixture. Cover and chill the dough for 2 to 3 hours.

❀ Preheat oven to 375 degrees.

❀ On a lightly floured board, shape the dough with your hands to form 4 flat loaves that are about 1/2 inch thick, 2 inches wide and as long as your cookie sheets. Butter cookie sheets. Place no more than 2 loaves on each cookie sheet. Bake for approximately 15 to 20 minutes. When removed from oven, loaves should be raised and just beginning to brown. The centers need to be cooked but not dry. Leave oven on.

❀ Let loaves cool on pans until comfortable to touch. Using a sharp knife, cut into diagonal slices 1/2 to 3/4 inch thick. Place slices on cut sides close together on same cookie sheet and return to hot oven for approximately 10 minutes. Check to watch browning and turn to toast other side for just a few minutes. Watch closely. Cool on wire racks before storing.

❀ Makes about 9 dozen cookies.

Kitchen Sink Cookies

Ingredients:

4	sticks butter
2	cups sugar
2	cups brown sugar
3	cups flour
2	teaspoons baking powder
2	teaspoons baking soda
4	eggs
1	teaspoon vanilla
1	cup nuts, chopped
2	cups oatmeal
2	cups Wheaties cereal
2	cups Rice Krispies cereal
2	cups coconut, shredded
1	package (12-ounce) semi-sweet chocolate chips
1	cup raisins

❀ Preheat oven to 350 degrees.

❀ In a very large bowl, mix sugars and butter together. In a small bowl, mix flour, baking powder and soda; add to sugar and butter mixture. Add one egg at a time and blend well; add vanilla and each of remaining ingredients one at a time and mix well. Shape dough into golf ball-size portions and bake for 10 to 12 minutes on ungreased cookie sheets.

❀ Makes 5 dozen.

The Chumskie Curse

At work the small group of engineers used to celebrate their birthdays by having the most recent celebrant supply the goodies for the next one. That way, everyone could play host. When Kimberly's birthday came around, Joe Everett presented her with a big box of chocolate chip cookies which turned out to be the most scrumptious morsels she had ever tasted. Joe called them Chumskie's Chocolate Chunks, and promised to get the recipe from his wife for his colleague. Kimberly couldn't wait to get her hands on the recipe and replace the one she had been using, which had been rewarding her with nondescript, flat, and slightly greasy cookies.

Joe appeared at work the next day with a sad look on his face, and informed Kimberly that his wife could not give him the recipe. Ridiculous as it might sound, she insisted that there was a kind of curse connected with the handing over to strangers of the secret ingredients. The cookie carried the Chumskie curse — from some Transylvania ancestor — she warned. How romantic! A cookie with a curse? Now Kimberly wanted that recipe more than ever, and beleaguered Joe with bribes and pleas.

The following day he stopped at Kimberly's office, smiling smugly from ear to ear as he dropped a crumpled piece of paper on her desk. She was now the proud owner of a cookie recipe with a curse!

When she asked him what kind of bribe he had used to entice his wife to hand over the treasure, he said she had done no such thing. "I know where she keeps her recipes. When she was asleep, I simply went to the kitchen and stole it."

What heroism! May the curse be a blessed one — may Chumskie be fond of rich, delicious chocolate chunk cookies.

Kimberly sets out a plate for Chumskie's ghost each time she bakes a batch of chunks. She claims the plate is empty in the morning!

Chumskie's Chocolate Chunk Cookies

Ingredients:

2	sticks butter, softened
1	cup white sugar
1	cup lightly packed brown sugar
2	eggs
1	teaspoon vanilla
2	cups flour
1	teaspoon baking powder
1	teaspoon baking soda
1/2	teaspoon salt
2-1/2	cups oatmeal, powdered (see instructions)
1	bag (6-ounce) semi-sweet chocolate chips
1	bag (12-ounce) plain milk chocolate jumbo-size chips
1	cup walnuts, chopped (optional)

- ❀ Preheat oven to 350 degrees.
- ❀ Powdered oatmeal:
  Render oatmeal powder-fine by placing in food processor or blender on low speed for 2 minutes. (Measure 2-1/2 cups whole oatmeal before powdering).
- ❀ Cream together butter, brown sugar and white sugar. Add eggs and vanilla. In a separate bowl combine flour, baking powder, baking soda, salt and powdered oatmeal. Add chocolate chips and nuts and mix well. Form small balls of dough and place on a lightly greased cookie sheet, bake for approximately 10 minutes. Do not overbake.
- ❀ Makes about 3 dozen cookies.

One Bite For You, Two For Me…Three For Me, Four…

Dee and her husband, John, attended a neighborhood block party several summers ago. Each resident brought something to contribute to the feast. Dee decided to bring her delicious Chocolate Kahlua dessert, knowing full well what a showpiece it was. She was also aware of the fact that the rich dessert had been her husband's downfall every time she prepared it. John was hooked on sweets, and especially that one.

She placed the cake in her prettiest Waterford crystal bowl and delivered it to the dessert table. True to form, John was the first to go through the dessert line and took a taste of each of the sweet treats. Evidently he enjoyed his wife's contribution so much that he proceeded to carry around the beautiful bowl with its serving spoon, taking a little nibble here, a bigger taste there, and big swallows standing still. Dee was mortified when she realized her darling had polished off the Chocolate Kahlua treat which was intended to feed at least part of the neighborhood residents.

That was not the end of the story. It happened again when Dee made the famous dessert for visitors as her after-dinner surprise, and she was foiled again. She caught John and a friend red-handed standing over the bowl with spoons in hand, scraping the sides for the last of the last bits.

Hey, to heck with the rest of the group!

Ingredients:

1	chocolate fudge cake (prepared package) with necessary ingredients to bake
1	large package (5.9-ounce) instant chocolate pudding (3 cups prepared) with necessary ingredients to prepare
1	large container whipped topping
6	large Heath bars
1/2	cup Kahlua

Chocolate Kahlua Dessert

❀ Freeze Heath bars. Prepare pudding according to directions, turn into bowl and chill. Bake cake according to directions in a 9 X 13 inch pan and cool thoroughly before assembling dessert.

❀ Remove candy wrappers, place candy bars in sturdy plastic bag, pound with a mallet or hammer to crumble into small pieces. Break cake into big pieces and line the bottom of your prettiest crystal bowl with about a third of it. Sprinkle with Kahlua. Spread a layer of pudding over cake pieces; add layer of Cool Whip, add candy pieces. Repeat 2 more times for a total of three layers. Chill and spoon onto plates to serve.

❀ Serves 6 to 8 (or one husband).

It Was a Dark and Stormy Night

Virginia's sister-in-law served a delicious fruit pizza one evening, and everybody just loved it. Virginia's kids asked her several times to make it, so she asked her sister-in-law, Jean, for the recipe. Jean announced that she didn't give out recipes. That came as quite a shock to Virginia. Jean had been a member of the family for a couple of years, and both Virginia and her mother had shared recipes with Jean in the past. Rather irked, Virginia let it go for the time being.

Several months later, Virginia was staying overnight at her brother's place for some reason that she can't remember now. The dark and ominous clouds that had gathered at the end of day had culminated in a heavy storm. Lightening flashed and sharp claps of thunder turned into rumbling roarings, and awakened Virginia in the middle of the night. She had gotten up to close the windows in her room, when a bolt of lightning flashed in her mind. She tiptoed into the kitchen, quietly rummaged around Jean's recipe stash, found the one she was looking for and, by the light of a digital clock and an occasional streak of lightning, copied it quickly on a paper towel.

Virginia gets a special delight serving this delightful dessert, and she still gets quite a kick out of the unsavory way she managed to take possession of this tasty dish. However, she is careful never to have it around when her sister-in-law is present.

Fruit Pizza

Ingredients:

Dough:

3	tablespoons shortening
1-1/2	cups flour
2	teaspoons baking powder
1	teaspoon salt
3/4	cup milk

Topping:

3	cups apples, sliced
1/2	cup sugar
1/2	teaspoon cinnamon
1/4	cup butter, melted

☙ Preheat oven to 425 degrees.
☙ Mix all the dough ingredients together, spread on a pizza pan or cookie sheet.
☙ Mix apples with sugar and cinnamon, arrange in rows on top of dough. Drizzle butter over the pizza. Bake for 20 to 30 minutes.
☙ Serves 6 to 8.

☙ For a "Fourth of July" pizza with that patriotic red-white-and-blue look, alternate circles of strawberries, blueberries and pale Thompson seedless grapes (halved). Use any other fruit or combination of fruit for a colorful presentation.

Index

Stolen Recipes and Saucy Stories
List of Contributors

"If I don't have friends, then I ain't got nothin'."
Billie Holiday

Carol Alexander
Julie Ammann
Kaye Allen
Debra Amren
Hollie Andrews
Martha Ellie Avegno
Ursula Bacon
Tracy Bair
Chris Bear
Virginia Bittler
Diane Bliquez
Melinda Buckle
Debbie Buckle
Kelly Casey
Melissa Chassaignac
Amy Clancy
Joy Crump
Liza Delacey
Nancy Duke
Kelly Egeck
Lori Ehrig
Marilyn Faherty
Charlene Florian
Maria Ponzi-Fogelstrom

Mary Foster
Michelle Fritts
Sandy Gannett
Catherine Gerlach
Martha Gerlicher
Colleen Gillis
Dee Goliwas
Mary Goodman
Norma Harper
Cara Henry
Kim Horton
Laila Kaiser
Susie Keeton
Stephanie Kersten
Marilyn Kessler
Cindy Kingsbury
Kim Kobata
Juile Lee
Laurie Lowe
Mary Jane Lowe
Peggy Lumpkin
Nancy McDaniel
Lynn Mesher
Ellen Middleton
Lyn Mills

Beth Morse
Carol Lee Morse
Kay Morse
Alicia O'Neill
Wendy Paisley
Jackie Peterson
Barbara Rodway
Kimberly Sanquist
Nikki Schroeder
Cathy Tacke
Pamela Tacke
Lisa Torkelson
Keith Tulloch
Kirsten Wagner
Laurie Weigel
Debbie Williamson

To order additional copies of

Stolen Recipes
and
Saucy Stories

Book: $19.95   Shipping/Handling $3.50

Contact: **BookPartners, Inc.**
P.O. Box 922, Wilsonville, OR 97070
Fax: 503-682-8684
Phone 503-682-9821
Phone: 1-800-895-7323